Making Mantels

Making Mantels

BY DAVID GETTS

LINDEN PUBLISHING
FRESNO, CA

MAKING MANTELS

Text © 2002 by David Getts
Photographs © 2002 by David Getts

Illustrations © 2002 David Getts: Figures 27, 28, 31, 32, 33, 34, 36, 40, 41, 88, 89, 90, 91, 129, 130, 181, 182, 183, 184, 185, 186, 187, 216, 230, 231, 248, 302, 305, 306, 315, 318, 320, 321, 335, 339, 340, 341, 342, 343.

Illustrations © Linden Publishing: 1, 2, 3, 4, 5, 6, 7, 8, 9, 10, 11, 12, 13, 14, 15, 16, 17, 18, 19, 20, 21, 22, 23, 24, 25, 26, 42, 44, 48, 49, 50, 51, 52, 53, 54, 55, 56, 57, 58, 59, 60, 61, 62, 63, 65, 66, 67, 69, 70, 71, 72, 73, 74, 75, 76, 77, 78, 79, 80, 194, 195, 198, 200, 201, 202, 203, 208, 211, 243, 319, 324, 325, 328, 345, 352.

ISBN 0-941936-72-4
2 4 6 8 9 7 5 3
First printing: August 2002
Printed in Singapore
Library of Congress Cataloging-in-Publication Data

Getts David, 1959-
  Making mantels / by David Getts.
    p. cm.
Includes bibliographical references and index.
  ISBN 0-941936-72-4 (paperback : alk. paper)
  1. Mantels. I. Title.
  TH2288.G48 2002
  684.1'6--dc21

2002007194

Your safety is your responsibility. Neither the author nor the publisher assume any responsibility for any injuries suffered or for damages or other losses incurred that may result from material presented in this publication.

Additional art by James Goold.

LINDEN PUBLISHING

The Woodworker's Library ®

Linden Publishing Inc.
2006 S. Mary St.
Fresno, CA 93721 USA
tel 800-345-4447
www.lindenpub.com

TABLE OF CONTENTS

Acknowledgments

W E ARE ONLY AS GOOD AS THE PEOPLE
we surround ourselves with. Without the help of the following people, I
would not have been able to put this book together.

First and foremost I would like to thank my wife, Lori. Without her endless
patience, encouragement, and support, I would not have been able to endure. I also
wish to thank my son, Tyler, for reminding me of the important things in life, and
my daughter, Emily, for her abundant supply of pencils!

A special note of thanks goes to Michael G. Walters Photography for the hard
work and many hours spent on photographing this work. All photos are by Michael
G. Walters. except those on pages 92, 93 and 94, which I took myself.

In addition, I would like to thank the people who helped collect information and
those who opened their homes to photographing: Mr. & Mrs. Greg Smith, Mr. &
Mrs. Herman van Deursen, Mr. & Mrs. Dana McDonald, Mr. & Mrs. Al Patey, Mr.
& Mrs. David Duce, Mr. and Mrs. Ken Pascoe, Mr. & Mrs. Marc Portsmith, Mr. &
Mrs. Jim Armstrong, Mr. & Mrs. Martin Dafforn, Mr. & Mrs. James Maher, Diane
Wells of the Diocesan House (Leary Mansion), Greg Watson of the Marymoor
Museum (Clise Mansion), Larry Kreisman of Historic Seattle, Northwest Mantel of
Kirkland, WA, Craig Sawyer of Craig Sawyer Designs, The Sorrento Hotel, and The
Stimson-Green Mansion.

Last and absolutely not least, I would like to thank God, who has privileged me
with the breath of life. ●

Introduction

THE FIRST MANTEL I BUILT WAS over 20 years ago. It was a simple shelf with two corbel supports. At the time I thought that was all a mantel was. Although I had seen ornate mantel surrounds, I had not yet developed an appreciation for them. It wasn't until I received my first commission to build a full mantel surround that I took notice. I began to see all the elements that show a woodworker's prowess: mouldings, frame-and-panel construction, carvings, matched veneered paneling, and specialty finishes. Coupled with that was the coalescent beauty of wood sharing space with the stone mason's craftsmanship. As with just about any subject, you don't realize how little you know until you start researching it.

Learning about a subject is the beginning of enlightenment. I've had clients who have hired me to build them a cabinet. Through the education process of design, learning about materials, and technique, they eventually came to understand it's not just an object they will receive, but an experience. Seeing a craftsman ply his trade in the creation of an object made specifically for them forever changes how they view the craft. Knowledge of a subject heightens your appreciation.

But acquiring knowledge in the learning process is not enough. Applying what you've learned is the next logical step. Each individual processes knowledge differently. Therefore, how you apply what you've learned could be in the form of building a mantel or simply enhancing your enjoyment of mantels. The intent of this book is to be a stepping stone–part of the learning and application process.

Building mantels has always been a source of joy for me. Seeing the work of other craftsmen has complemented this joy. Whether they are simple or complex, mantels express both the builder's creativity and the homeowner's lifestyle. You don't have to build a mantel to benefit from its warmth. But building one increases your appreciation because of what you've learned.

HOW TO USE THIS BOOK

The material in this book is divided into conventional chapters to guide readers through the process of designing and building a mantel. However, when constructing a mantel, it would be a mistake to become trapped in the linear format of the book. While it's logical to assume that, for the most comprehensive understanding, the information in Chapter 1 should precede the information in Chapter 2, I caution you that this assumption is relevant only to reading. In actual construction, things are often different. For example, you may require a better understanding of materials (discussed in Chapters 4 and 5) before you can address the design issues presented in Chapter 2. Or understanding how to install the finished project (covered in Chapter 10) may precede the decision of whether you will prefinish the mantel in the shop or on the job site (Chapter 9). Therefore, keep an open mind that in the designing and building process understanding a final step in fabrication may very well come before dealing with a beginning step in design. •

1. Early homes relied exclusively on the fireplace for both heating and cooking. The fire surround often consisted of a simple mantel shelf with corbels or a cornice.

CHAPTER 1

A Brief History of Mantels

IN THIS DISCUSSION I WILL HIGHLIGHT only selected aspects of the mantel's evolution, not specific detail changes. Nonetheless, it's worth attending to the roots of the mantel's development, since these basics will support the fruit that is borne on your project.

A mantel is defined as the whole of the finish around a fireplace. This includes the chimney breast covering in front (and sometimes on both sides), the shelf above a fireplace, and even the lintel–the beam, stone, or arch that supports the masonry above a fireplace. As shown in the illustration on Page 16, mantels can include all or any combination of the elements above. In addition, the elements used to adorn or embellish the fireplace opening, including freestanding stoves, all fit within the definition of "mantel."

2. Overmantels, the decorative work above the mantel shelf, were popular during the 17th century.

The 17th century brought further refinement to fireplace mantels. Although some homes still contained only a brick fireplace outfitted with a bake oven, many fireplaces were far more elaborate. The expensive and ornamental use of materials and craftsmanship often displayed the occupation or interests of an owner and were a sign of prestige. Overmantels (Chapter 2) were often sculpted to contain naturalistic themes of animals and plants, religious symbols, or story-telling elements. When hoods for collecting smoke were used, even they were often adorned to match the other elements. Chimneyboards—ornamental boards placed in front of the firebox during summer months to stop drafts and no doubt to conceal the dirty firebox—were introduced during this period. These were usually painted to complement the mantel; some designs even incorporated shutters.

During the 18th century, the Georgian architectural style (1690-1800) became popular. This style was characterized by tall mantel shelves, large pilasters, and overmantels that reached the ceiling. Because coal began to replace wood as fuel, metal grates for burning coal began to replace andirons. But unlike the metal grates that are common today, 18th-century grates, like the andirons before them, were highly ornamental and expensive—a statement of the importance our ancestors placed upon the fireplace. Clearly, the fireplace was rapidly becoming the visual centerpiece of the home. Expensive mantels

From the time that fire was first harnessed for use in the dwelling place, the mantel has enjoyed the spotlight. In early homes, if there was one fireplace, the room it served was both kitchen and living room and typically was the heart of the home. Early fireplaces were often made of a wood frame with decorative plaster or mud infill. Early mantels consisted of a simple stone or wood lintel, and although many early wood lintels have stood the test of time, they would certainly cause heart palpitations in

your local building official today.

During the 16th century the wall fireplace became extremely popular. Because the fireplace was used for heat, it was always centrally located, and so it was natural for the fireplace to become a point of architectural interest. Thus began the move toward more decorative treatments. Even utilitarian firebacks and andirons (discussed in Chapter 2) served ornamental as well as practical purposes, and were used to display the status or allegiances of the homeowner.

could be made from carved whited statuary marble inlayed with colored marble. Less expensive options might include wood with carved or applied details. Private or utility room mantels were typically plain.

As the kitchen became separated from the social areas, the fireplace continued to mark the social center of the household. Rooms and even whole houses were designed around the fireplace wall. Closets, doors, and cupboards were commonly grouped around this vital heat source. Other notable trends of the time included smaller fireplace openings, decorative plaster overmantel treatments, faux marble and other inlays, and horizontal and vertical ribbed decorations. The placement of one or more mirrors in an overmantel was a sign of great wealth. Not readily available and extremely expensive, mirrors were a good choice At the end of the 18th century, there was a move toward using straight, rather than curvilinear, lines in mantel design. In addition, wood-burning stoves became more common as heat sources.

The 19th century continued to see the mantel's place in the home further defined. Federal-style (1780-1830) features were simpler, had more delicate moldings, and narrower pilasters. Although there was a continued use of traditional materials for creating classical motifs, new materials like blue and white earthenware tiles were gaining popularity as slips. Few mantel designs were available in the early part of the century because most

3. During the latter part of the 19th century mantels were becoming functional as well as decorative. Built-in bookcases or display nooks were commonly integrated into the design.

mantels were probably purchased from manufacturers. Pattern-book designs emerged later and had an influence on design. It was during the 19th century that the mantel shelf became more distinct. Its depth increased, presumably as more home accessories, such as mantel clocks and candle holders, became available.

Victorian period (1837-1910) homes placed a great value on the fireplace, and some had a fireplace in every room. One-piece castings of inner frame, fireback, grate, and

damper (much like a modern day fireplace insert), were making fires more efficient. Large homes were still using marble and slate for mantels. Painted or finished wood mantels were being used in smaller homes or the secondary rooms of larger houses. Complete cast-iron mantel surrounds could also be purchased. Built-in cabinets or cupboards were being designed around mantels. Elaborate ornamentation-including spindle work, dark woodwork, and a mix of various styles-was commonly found

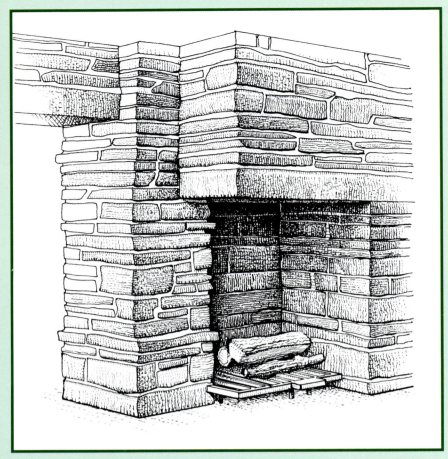

4. Designing with stone is popular in any era.

in this period. Heating was important to Americans, but even when centralized heating made fireplaces technologically obsolete, they were not abandoned. The fireplace and mantel, including overmantels, display shelves, seating, and a place to display art, remained a symbol of social status and wealth.

The latter part of the 19th century saw even greater changes in mantel design. Using marble slips with a wood surround, a common design today, had already proven to be more cost-effective than incorporating a full marble surround. Tile was another less costly alternative. Tile was available in many colors and patterns, was as

durable as stone, and was easy to clean—a cost-effective material. In addition, mirrors were becoming more affordable, which increased their use. Gas fires arrived toward the end of the century, but were expensive and not immediately well received. They would not become a factor until the 20th century.

The early 20th century ushered in the Arts & Crafts movement (1860-1926). Plain stone or brick chimneys typified this style. The use of tile for slips increased, and inglenooks, or sitting areas by a fireplace, were introduced. Inglenooks were not always small and intimate. Some affluent homes had large nooks that were more

like separate rooms than cozy hideaways.

Even as heating and cooking technology advanced, fireplaces clothed with a mantel still symbolized the heart of the home. But they were now free of functional requirements and could be designed strictly to make a statement. Gas fireplace heaters became more efficient. The availability of different materials led to further design evolution. For example, ornate glazed tiles were on the rise. There was also an increased use of painted cast-iron mantel surrounds. Their relative low cost, along with the ability to feature ornate shapes and designs, made them a popular choice and brought elegance into more homes.

During the 1930s, the pendulum swung back from ornate workmanship to simpler designs: rectangular openings, a plain hearth slab, and chrome or other metal edging. Even the mantel shelf was removed from its traditional location and placed elsewhere on the wall. Electric fires in a streamlined surround were competing well against gas because they were less obtrusive. The focus was clearly shifting toward a less prominent role for the fireplace. But the fireplace was still deemed an important part of the house due to its continued popularity and as a way to sell space. This was the period of illuminated niches in the chimneybreast, stepped and asymmetrical use of brick and stone, and flat stone or tile set flush to the wall.

By the 1950s, America was coming out of a world war. The

combination of the baby boom and more conservative building practices changed how fireplaces and decorative mantels were viewed. Entire fireplace walls of rugged stone became popular, as did built-in bookcases and nooks for wood storage. But during the 1950s, the use of free-standing wood stoves began to redefine the fireplace. As technological improvements made wood stoves relatively inexpensive—and more efficient—to purchase and use, cost-conscious consumers snapped them up. In these cases, the mantel tended to be pushed aside for more practical uses of the house construction budget.

The latter part of the 20th century saw the mantel return to popularity, a trend that continues today thanks in part to advances in technology that make mantels more affordable. Innovations in manufactured fireplaces have made them less costly, which leaves more room in the budget for decorative millwork. Wood, pellet, and gas-log fireplace inserts are breathing new life into antiquated fireplaces. Interest in these alternate heating sources is rejuvenating the mantel's prominence. In addition, the greater availability of plastic moldings, cast-plaster products, and solid-surface materials (such as Corian and Gibralter), are making ornate work more affordable. Even computers play a role, in that they help simplify labor-intensive detail work. Many old mantels in homes and salvage yards are being restored as interest in these gems of millwork increase.

As society continues to advance

5. Conservative building practices of the 1950s reduced the mantel's importance. Fireboxes were often minimized with flat walls and simple slips.

technologically, the tendency is to leave behind old practices. New materials and methods seem to push aside older practices, even making them obsolete. With that said, we must never view craftsmanship in the rear-view mirror. The ornate mantels of old were fabricated by skilled craftsman. Only the wealthy could afford them. The advent of new technology (not to mention resourceful people), will allow more people to be comforted by the soft glow of a fire dancing on mantel pilasters. The majority of homes today rely on central heat, which could cause the fireplace mantel to lose its luster if it were not for that certain something that a fireplace adds to a home. As for mantels, they offer just as much opportunity for expression as they ever did. In addition, fireplaces and mantels remain a symbol of our roots, constantly reminding us of our dependence on fire for sustaining basic survival. Mantels also chronicle how we have developed as a society. When properly executed, the fireplace and mantel can demand a place as a home's focal point and certainly serve, as they did from earliest days, as the heartbeat of the home. ⊙

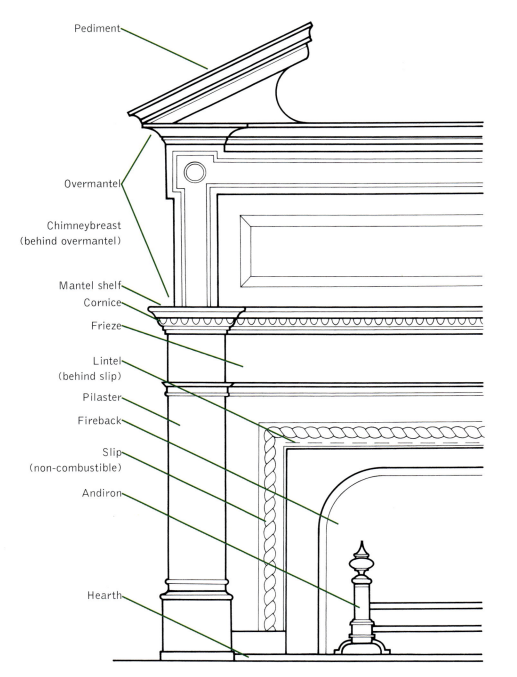

Pediment

Overmantel

Chimneybreast
(behind overmantel)

Mantel shelf
Cornice
Frieze

Lintel
(behind slip)

Pilaster

Fireback

Slip
(non-combustible)

Andiron

Hearth

Pediment tops overmantel.

Overmantel is any
decorative work
(panels, molding,
painting, mirror,
etc.) that extends
above basic mantel
surround.

Corbels may top each jamb to
support cornice, and are
usually decorative.

Lintel supports stone or
brickwork above firebox.

Jambs (vertical legs) are
called pilasters when they
project from wall.

Frieze, or header, connects
pilasters.

The non-combustible slip
surrounds firebox on three sides.

Hearth, made of non-
combustible material, may be
flush with floor or raised.

6. All mantels share some or all of these common parts.

CHAPTER *2*

Mantel Design

THE FIRST RULE IN MANTEL DESIGN is that fireplaces should be beautiful even when there is no fire. The number of hours a modern fireplace burns in one year could probably be counted on two hands. The second rule is that all rules can be broken, except the first rule. When designing, don't limit yourself–learning to be creative relies on mastering the basic principles and then following your instinct. Most people can tell when a design is nicely proportioned or balanced even when not professionally trained. That is design instinct. Principles are the knowledge you need to make intelligent decisions about materials, function, and surrounding elements as they pertain to a mantel. In other words, instinct is what you use to confirm the choices you have made based on the principles you have used. For instance, if you follow the suggestions in this chapter and other design books, you may design a mantel that is technically correct in form and function, yet somehow misses the mark. When designing, it's crucial to consider all surrounding non-architectural elements, including such things as artwork, furniture, lifestyle, and the view you have out the window.

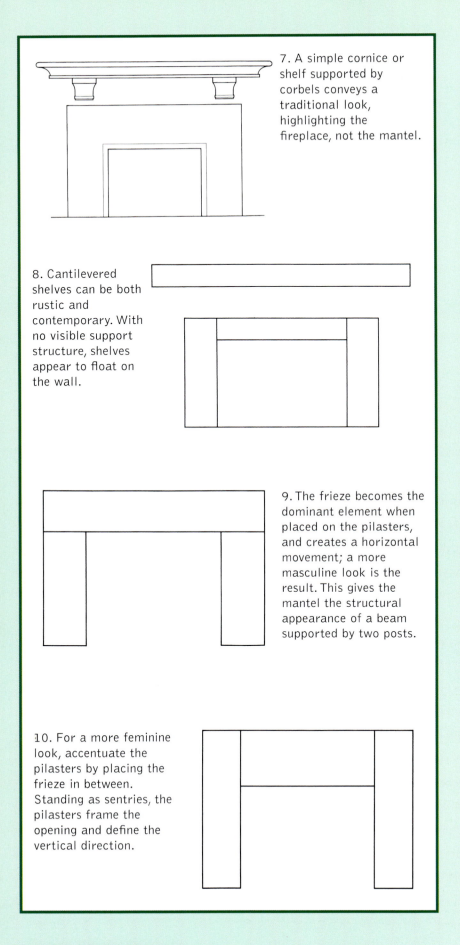

7. A simple cornice or shelf supported by corbels conveys a traditional look, highlighting the fireplace, not the mantel.

8. Cantilevered shelves can be both rustic and contemporary. With no visible support structure, shelves appear to float on the wall.

9. The frieze becomes the dominant element when placed on the pilasters, and creates a horizontal movement; a more masculine look is the result. This gives the mantel the structural appearance of a beam supported by two posts.

10. For a more feminine look, accentuate the pilasters by placing the frieze in between. Standing as sentries, the pilasters frame the opening and define the vertical direction.

One should approach design as both looking through a telescope and a microscope. With the telescope you look at elements far away or beyond your own home or life for ideas. Magazines, books, museums, and anything outside your milieu can offer design options. Looking through the microscope helps you identify both the architectural and non-architectural features that are currently a part of your life. Linking these two viewpoints can radically change your approach to design.

I will not attempt to give readers a course in design, but rather to highlight some principles to get you started. Because design is limited by a number of restrictions (pre-determined dimensions to work with, the safe placement of combustible materials, and standard sizes of materials among other issues), mantels are relatively easy to design. Still, they demand careful attention. The placement of mantel parts and their relationship to one another can radically effect design. For example, cornices are typically supported by either pilasters or corbels (Figure 7); this is how you achieve a traditional look. Because the cornice has to share space with the other elements, its importance is reduced. If it stands alone, it will take on the appearance of an inadequately supported beam (Figure 8). A shelf cantilevered in this way has less mass and is more contemporary in appearance. If the frieze is supported by the pilasters (Figure 9), it looks more like a beam being held up by two posts. This approach emphasizes the frieze more than the pilasters. By contrast, if the frieze is placed between the pilasters (Figure 10), it takes on a less significant visual role. Pilasters that run up to the cornice will demand more attention than the frieze.

Design is easiest to handle if broken down into three phases. Conceptualization, or the idea, is your first step. This is followed by discovery, which can be likened to research and development. Since this is the stage at which you develop your ideas, too much research is better than not enough. The last phase is fabrication, or the implementation of the design.

Before the design process can continue, you need to have a pretty good idea of the type of materials you are going to use. Chapter 4 discusses the choices of wood. Chapter 5 covers the use of non-combustible and other materials. Chapter 9 explains staining, finishing, and painting, which can greatly affect design. At this stage it's not imperative that you decide on every material. Just make certain that you have considered all the available options. That way, if you are still undecided, you will at least have enough information to proceed with the actual design work. In addition, the more research you do initially, the less regret you may encounter later when you find you're not able to add an embellishment because you didn't allow for it earlier.

FORMING A CONCEPT

Developing a concept starts with observation. Take time to examine the house for some direction on styling. If you have a 1920s Craftsman-style home, you cer-

tainly won't want to create a mantel with a contemporary design. Juxtaposition (placing differing design styles and elements side by side), can create visual interest, but in the afore-mentioned example, it simply does not work. A mantel will become a fixture, part of the house's millwork. Don't botch the home designer's original intent by introducing elements that don't belong. Older homes typically have more woodwork, so a careful study of the style and use of moldings should give you a clear starting point. Contemporary homes generally lack woodwork so your options will actually be broader.

WOOD

Note the type of wood in the home. Is it rustic knotty pine or furniture-quality cherry? Don't mix woods that aren't complementary. While different species look lovely when placed side by side, some woods just don't appreciate being in the same room together. Maybe you have painted millwork. Either painted or clear-finished mantels go well with both clear-finished and painted millwork.

THE CHIMNEYBREAST

Are you dealing with brick, stone, or drywall? And is your plan to cover the existing material or accentuate it? Brick, a common material, can be so visually dominant that clients often ask me to tone down an overwhelming wall of brick. "Cover as much as you can," they say. Fortunately, most brick is flat and covering it is fairly straightforward. Brick veneer typically projects from the wall the

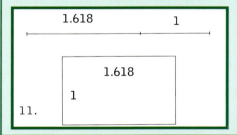

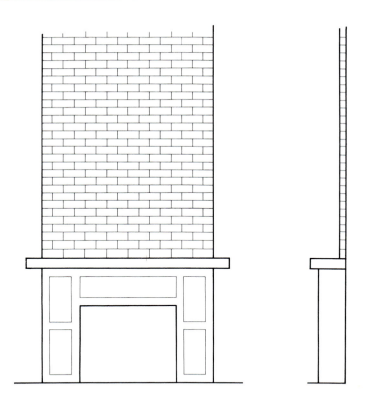

12. Totally covering the brick on the bottom allows the mantel to stand alone as its own design element. The brick wall above must submit to or complement the mantel's design.

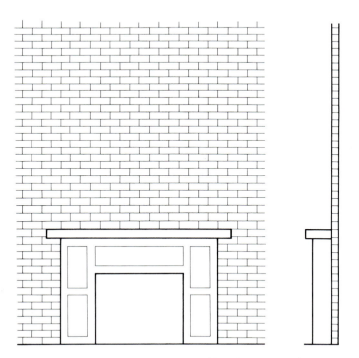

13. Building a mantel on a wall of brick will not diminish the dominant brick features. This example shows how the mantel becomes a supporting member of the brick wall theme.

thickness of the brick. If the brick is located only at the fireplace chimney, all the brick under the mantel shelf can easily be covered by the mantel surround (see Figure 12). If, however, the brick extends the entire width of a room, you may elect to provide only a basic surround (see Figure 13). I have enclosed entire brick walls by creating a wood paneling, but this must be designed into the mantel surround to maintain continuity.

Stone is similar to brick in its stable appearance, but is usually given more latitude or leniency in design because it is a natural element. In fact, river-rock fireplaces look best with just a simple cornice shelf. There is no need to muddle a fireplace design with a mantel that doesn't belong. Don't feel that you have to create a masterpiece to be successful. Sometimes less is best.

Drywall and plaster walls are the easiest to design around. Since most are flat and lack design interest in themselves, they offer the mantel designer many choices. When I'm faced with a flat plaster wall I usually try to find nearby elements to incorporate into the mantel. This helps to tie the new work into the old.

THE HEARTH

What type of hearth do you have? If it is flush to the floor you won't have any restrictions when planting the pilaster legs. By contrast, a raised hearth, which can be anywhere from 1 inch to 24 inches off the floor, will require deliberate decisions on how and where to place the pilasters.

Three design issues arise when fitting a mantel to a hearth. The pilaster legs can either sit on, split, or span the hearth. Sitting pilasters rest entirely on the hearth (Figure 14); splitting pilasters overlap both the hearth and surrounding floor (Figure 15); and spanning pilasters are on the outside of the hearth (Figure 16). If you are retrofitting an existing fireplace, you may have no choice in how the mantel joins the hearth. If this is a new construction project or a full-fledged remodel, you can dictate the choice. If possible, either have the pilaster sit completely on the hearth or span completely off the hearth. A mantel that splits a hearth can look like a building that slipped off its foundation, especially if it is a raised hearth. If your hearth is raised a few inches off the floor, you still have the three design options of sit, split, and span. Again, the sit and span methods work much better and are easier to construct. However, you may be constrained by existing conditions that require you to split the pilasters on a raised hearth (Figure 17). This situation will just require more creative design solutions.

What type, size, and shape of firebox do you have? If you live in an older home with a stone or brick firebox, you will want to consider those materials in the design process, particularly where the stone slip is concerned. Be sure to pick a non-combustible material that compliments the old, well-used firebox material. If, on the other hand, you have a metal prefabricated firebox, your stone

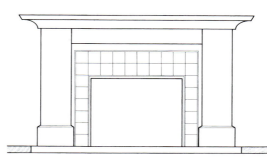

14. When a mantel sits entirely on the hearth, the non-combustible hearth defines the size. All of the mantel's elements, therefore, can be contained easily in the fireplace location.

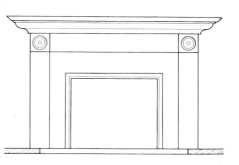

15. Splitting the pilasters forces the mantel to share space with both the finish flooring and the other elements in the room. Sometimes, differing floor materials can create problems with a pilaster sitting flush on the floor.

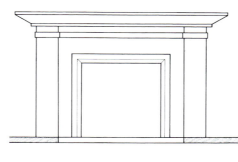

16. Pilasters that use the span method become independent of the hearth. The visual importance of the non-combustible slip is therefore reduced, allowing the mantel to dominate the firebox opening.

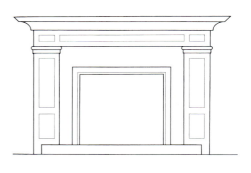

17. It's tough to ignore a raised hearth's visual impact. Raised hearths create design challenges, such as this "split" pilaster mantel.

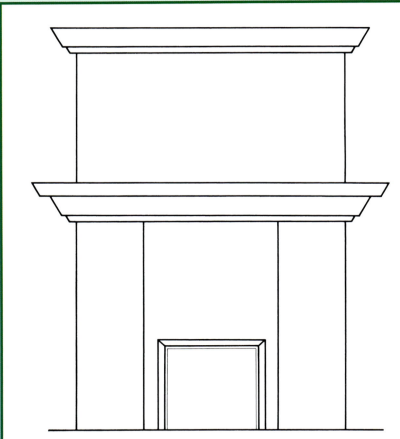

18. Poor design includes oversized mantels dwarfing a small firebox. When a large mantelpiece is desired, the illusion of firebox size can be changed by increasing the boundaries of the slip.

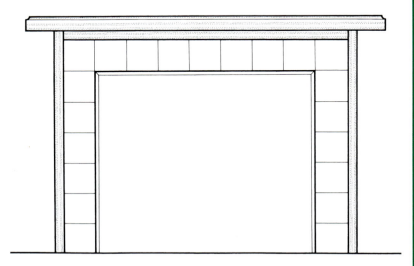

19. Although not as drastic a mistake as an oversized mantel, skimpy use of trims on a large firebox are pathetic executions in mantel design.

selection may be different. Metal combined with stone takes on a different appearance than stone with brick. The differences in texture between metal and stone, brick to stone, or other material combinations need to be analyzed before decisions can be made. The size of the firebox, although an obvious consideration, is often overlooked in design. It is assumed that the mantel must wrap around the opening, but don't neglect the actual size and shape of the firebox. Small fireboxes will be dwarfed by a large overmantel (Figure 18). Equally awkward is a large firebox with a skimpy mantel or shelf (Figure 19). Most fireboxes are rectangular in shape. Rectangles provide a good foundation from which the mantel can be built. Square fireboxes are rare, but can be found. A square box will require different proportions to look right. Arches and free-form firebox openings can either be tamed with a traditional look (Figure 20), or the mantel can follow the action of the box (Figure 21).

In addition to types of fireboxes you need to look at the type of fireplace you have. Are you building a mantel for an open box fireplace, a zero-clearance or a manufactured fireplace, a wood or gas insert, or a free-standing stove? All can be considered fireplaces, but each one is unique enough to require a different approach to designing a mantel. Each dictates a different attitude for the room and the mantel should reflect that. An open box fireplace gives you the greatest chance to create a traditional style of mantel. All the basic things we associate with a fireplace come with the open box construction: grate, stone slip, hearth, chimney, etc. These are the traditional things we have designed mantels around for centuries. Zero-clearance fireplaces, on the other hand, allow critical clearance dimensions to be stretched since combustible materials can be closer. With some sealed-gas models (no door), combustible material can be brought right up to the metal flange. Even though this can be done, should it? I'm not speaking in terms of safety but rather appearance. Mantels typically do not look right if they do not have a slip of some kind. In addition, prefabricated fireplaces are installed with insulated chimney pipe instead of brick. The pipe is concealed with a stud wall, or can be closed off with the mantel itself. Dollar savings are significant and the task of installing a brand new fireplace in an existing house is greatly simplified. As a designer, you must be aware that although these traditional fireplace elements (grate, stone slip, hearth, chimney, etc.) are not always required or needed with pre-fabricated fireplaces, they are an integral part of the traditional mantel.

Fireplace inserts can change the way a mantel looks. Study the design of the insert before planning the mantel. Look for key elements, like projection from the wall. Is the insert flush to the wall, giving it a more contemporary look, or does it sit out on the hearth like a stove? Does it have glass doors that open, or is it a sealed unit? Does it come in a

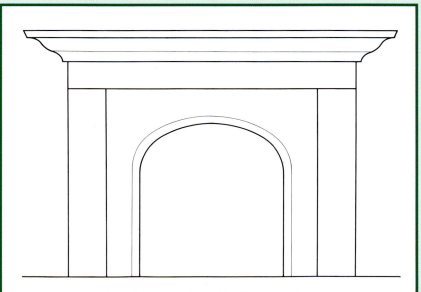

20. A straight frieze works well with an arched firebox if executed properly. Careful attention to proportion is the key to making this work.

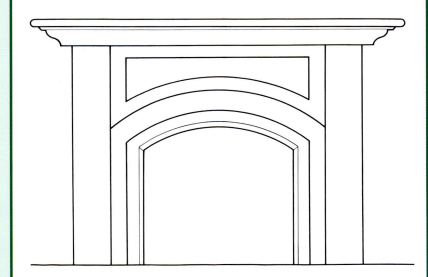

21. To accentuate the curve on a firebox, match the curve with the mantel frieze. Although more difficult to carry out, the results will be very rewarding.

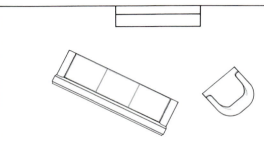

22. A fireplace in the middle of a large wall provides many options for design. Without space or location constraints, the designer is free to create the desired plan.

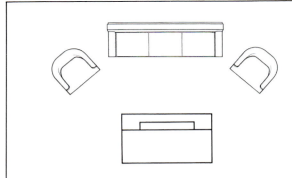

23. An island fireplace has four sides of the firebox to consider, instead of only the face. This type of fireplace is often used as a separation between two rooms. Does the mantel design take both rooms into consideration?

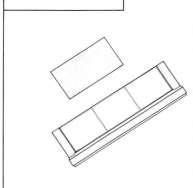

24. Providing balanced mantel design in a 90-degree corner fireplace is very challenging. Even when a symmetrical surround can be created, it's hard to ignore the feeling of being squeezed. Fortunately, this placement is rare.

matte black finish only, or are glossy colors available? Knowing specifications and restrictions will aid you in your design. For instance, if you want a mantel for a free-standing wood stove, you will be very limited. A shelf may be all you can do because the Uniform Building Codes prevent surrounding the stove with wood.

Other architectural elements, such as location, must be considered. Does the fireplace sit in the middle of a large, flat wall (Figure 22)? Is the fireplace wall set in the center of a room like an island (Figure 23)? Is the room set up with a 90-degree corner fireplace (Figure 24), or a 45-degree corner (Figure 25)? Each of these examples requires a different solution for the mantel design, even if the firebox, chimneybreast, and fireplace type were the same.

Wallboard material or other wall treatment should also be scrutinized. For instance, with a heavy, knock-down texture on your walls you may reconsider building a painted mantel with a smooth, high gloss epoxy finish. Or the trompe l'oeil wall above the fireplace may be covered by the overmantel you had your heart set on. Is the wall flat or does it return back on one or both sides, causing the fireplace to project even farther (Figure 26)? How tall is the ceiling? Do you really have room for the full surround you want? Is the fireplace in an upstairs room or basement? Are there windows to contend with? Windows, even when not in direct competition with the mantel, still must be considered as natural light creates a different feeling in a room. A room without windows will have a more private, den-like feeling that the mantel can echo. What sort of view do you have out your window?

Get a feel for your space before you sit down at the drawing board. You may see a mantel you like, but until you feel comfortable with the elements of the room, it will be difficult to determine if that design will flow. Decide what you like about the room and try to maintain those features. Let the introduction of a mantel accentuate the room or the house's architectural elements, not suppress them. Each room that houses a fireplace will tell you what the constraints are. You just need to be looking for them.

Buying a pre-made or antique mantel is another way to approach mantel design. All forms of art evoke emotion. When shopping for an antique desk you may find the perfect settee for your home. Certain objects speak to our hearts. It's as if they are crying out for us to adopt them. If that happens with your mantel project, don't feel guilty. There are some beautiful old mantels waiting to be restored and placed in a new home. In fact, I strongly encourage you to look at antiques and visit showrooms where custom mantels are built. It is in these places that you will glean some of the best ideas.

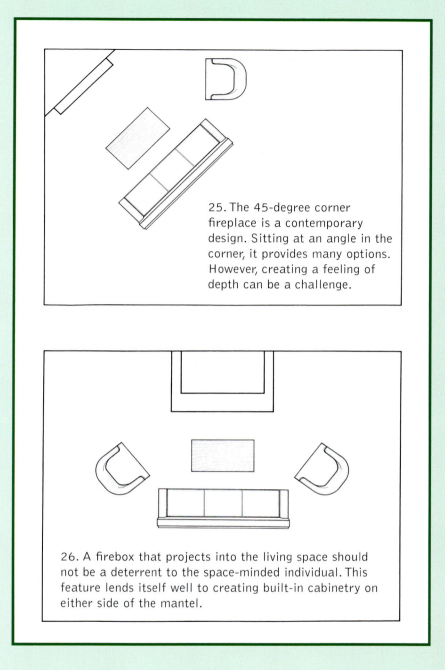

25. The 45-degree corner fireplace is a contemporary design. Sitting at an angle in the corner, it provides many options. However, creating a feeling of depth can be a challenge.

26. A firebox that projects into the living space should not be a deterrent to the space-minded individual. This feature lends itself well to creating built-in cabinetry on either side of the mantel.

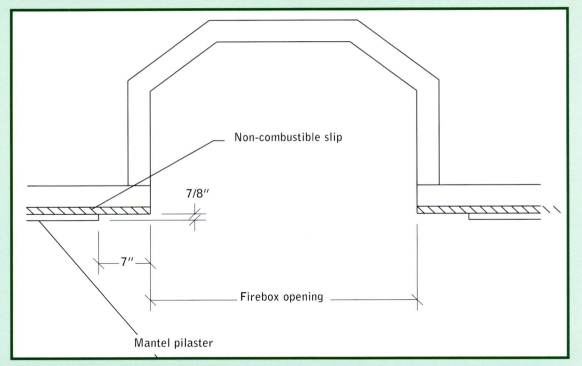

Non-combustible slip

7/8"

7"

Firebox opening

Mantel pilaster

27. Combustible material placed within 12 inches of the firebox opening is subject to the Uniform Building Code requirements of projection. In this example, the combustible material is 7 inches from the firebox opening. The Uniform Building Code stipulates 1/8-inch projection for every 1 inch from the firebox opening, resulting in a maximum 7/8-inch pilaster thickness.

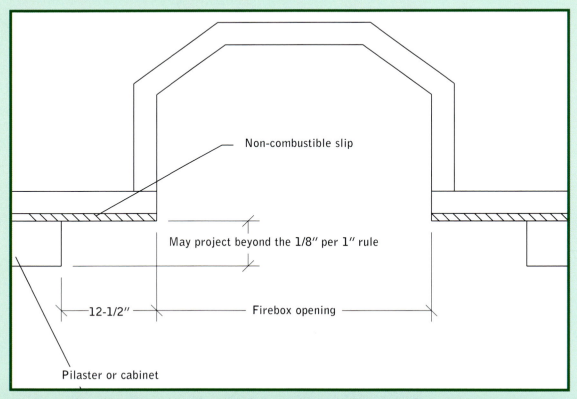

Non-combustible slip

May project beyond the 1/8" per 1" rule

12-1/2"

Firebox opening

Pilaster or cabinet

28. No combustible material can be placed closer than 6 inches to the firebox opening. Material 6 to 12 inches away is subject to the 1/8-inch projection rule. Combustible material that is farther than 12 inches may project beyond the 1/8 inch per 1 inch UBC rule, as this drawing shows.

THE ROLE OF SAFETY IN DESIGN

Mantel design has a very rigid side to it: designing a piece that will be beautiful and will be safe in a home. Placed close to a heat source, it must adhere to the Uniform Building Code's (UBC) requirements. Combustion is defined as: "Any chemical process accompanied by the emission of heat and light, typically by combination with oxygen." A combustible wall catches fire easily or conducts heat. This would include materials like plywood, solid wood, fiberboard, gypsum board, and plastics. In addition, paint and wood finishes are combustible.

The Uniform Building Codes (UBC) are very clear about keeping combustible materials away from the firebox opening. Section 3707 (h) states:

• Combustible material shall not be placed within 6 inches of the fireplace opening.

• No such combustible material within 12 inches of the fireplace opening shall project more than 1/8 inch for each 1-inch clearance from such opening.

If the pilasters are 7 inches away from the opening, their overall protrusion may not exceed 7/8 inch; i.e., 1/8 inch x 7 = 7/8 inch (Figure 27). This applies only to materials that are 12 inches or closer to the firebox. Combustible material that is placed beyond the 12-inch threshold is not subject to this rule (Figure 28).

Zero-clearance fireplaces and some other inserts may deviate from this rule if their design eliminates heat build-up. Be sure to check the manufacturer's specifications and those of your local building department.

BASIC DIMENSIONS

In addition to the UBC requirements, some basic guidelines to consider are listed below. These come to mind because there are few standard dimensions when planning a custom mantel, and every fireplace offers different challenges. However, some dimensions and proportions never seem to work. This should at least give you a foundation from which to start.

• 12 inches of non-combustible material are needed around the firebox (the slip). In addition to appearance, this provides two other advantages. First, the pilasters can project 1-1/2 inches from the wall (1/8 inch x 12). If you stretch the dimension beyond 12 inches, you can project the pilaster as much as you want. Second, many stone tiles are available in the 12-inch dimension.

• Pilaster width: 8 to 12 inches. This will depend largely on the pilaster detailing you choose.

• Frieze width: 8 to 16 inches. If possible, make the frieze wider than the pilasters. It lends a sense of permanence to the mantel. Less is good too, just avoid making the frieze and pilasters the same width.

• Cornice, 3 to 8 inches high. One or two-piece mouldings will give a narrow, simple look. Built-up mouldings will increase this dimension, lending more mass to the mantel.

• Shelf depth: 7 to 8 inches. This dimension will depend entirely upon the amount of bulk you add to the cornice, and the decided use of the shelf. For a standard shelf, 7 to 8 inches is a good proportion.

• Overmantels should be at least two-thirds the height of the lower mantel surround.

29. Full-size mock-ups help visualize what the mantel will look like. Simple cardboard versions like the one shown are easy to make and help the builder determine proportion and design compatibility.

DEVELOPING THE DESIGN

Whimsy is another approach to design. Whimsy is defined as "a freakish pattern of ideas and their associated emotions as a motive of action." Whimsy encourages you to throw caution to the wind and be gutsy. It takes the drudgery out of design work and makes it fun. This can produce both excellent and disastrous results. That is why I say to first follow instinct. You may feel you don't have a knack for design and therefore feel uncomfortable with whimsy. That is your instinct telling you to stay away from whimsy.

Another form of whimsy is bor-rowing. You see an element in another mantel, a piece of mill-work, a form that nature has pro-vided, or any other design you like, and you borrow that design and incorporate it into your proj-ect. Design is meant to be fun. Sometimes that means borrowing to create what you want. Think of all the artwork, movies, and music you have enjoyed that developed its roots by borrowing from some-thing or someone else. This is most easily achieved by research-ing for ideas. Keep your eyes open for fireplaces. See how others deal with fireplace surrounds. Borrow ideas that work with your house and plan. If you take the time to

look at other mantel details, you will quickly learn what you like and don't like. It's better to see and feel details. That way you get a sense of how the light reflects and casts shadows, something two-dimensional pictures fall short in providing. However, don't neglect books, as they usually point you in the direction of what to look for.

Others may feel creative but need help in design. This is when I encourage people to find a pro-fessional to design the piece. You can either be part of the design process or give carte blanche deci-sion-making to the designer. If someone else designs your piece you place the outcome of the project, as far as the design goes, into their hands. As long as you feel comfortable with this arrangement, you'll be fine. If, however, you plan to build the mantel but have someone else design it, you need to keep the design process open. You may need to change a designer's ideas because of availability of materials, tooling you have in your shop, woodworking skill level, and keeping to a realistic budget. Therefore, the builder is never totally removed from the design process.

After you have studied your home's architectural elements and looked around for other ideas, you should have a good feel for what details you like and what elements you are going to incorporate into the mantel. Traditional designs utilize crown mouldings, fluting, beading, raised panels, flat panels, plinth blocks, rosettes, dentil moulding, corbels, columns and capitols, applied mouldings, etc. (refer to chapter 5 for further explanation of materials). Most homes are complimented by a traditional design. With such a broad range of mouldings and fabrication techniques, most will blend with your architecture.

If your house is very modern, you may want to go another route. Contemporary designs are usually much simpler and meant to compliment the clean straight lines of a modern home. Elements often found in contemporary mantels include flat or gracefully curved pilasters, square-edged shelves, and the introduction of metals, stone, and whimsy. For a refresher on whimsy, think of Picasso. If you have forgotten what a work by Picasso looks like, find an art book and remind yourself. His work is considered modern art, and it leaves a lot to the imagination. In the case of mantel design, you are limited only by your imagination.

Once the mantel has been designed and drawn to scale, you have one more step before fabrication. Since dimensions and proportions don't always look the same on paper as they do full-sized in the real world, you may want to consider a full-size mock-up. This does not have to be a complicated, three-dimensional affair. I recommend a simple cardboard cut-out, with the design (flutes, panels, etc.) drawn on with a marker (Figure 29). Take the time to make it as close to scale as possible. This will greatly help you determine if your proportions are correct. It will also show how the elements you've chosen fit with the rest of the room.

This is the time to make changes. Usually your first instinct is correct, even if it's a whimsical one. You may want to leave the mock-up up for a few days to get a feel for it. Each day may evoke different feelings worth considering. Encourage others to critique your plan. Like the proverb says: "As iron sharpens iron, so one man sharpens another." Another person's opinions can be helpful. Just remember, it is just an opinion, not a directive. Only make changes that agree with the original design. •

30. Verifying conditions on a job site requires more than a tape measure. Items to consider including in the site inspection tool box are (from left bottom): sketch pad, utility knife, framing square, t-bevel, profile duplicator; (from top left) moulding samples, glue gun, cardboard, calculator, tape measure, tape, stud finder, and level.

CHAPTER 3

On-Site Inspection

INITIAL SITE INSPECTION SHOULD BE the very first task on your to-do list. You may have looked at your fireplace for ten years with the intent of building a mantel, but until you actually begin, you won't realize everything you need to know for design and construction. When I meet with potential clients about a project, my first trip to their home is simply to gather enough information (overall design concept, dimensions, etc.) to compile an estimate for the proposed project. Before design work can begin, I review existing conditions. How can you design something if you've never seen or studied the space? You can't. That's putting the cart before the horse. Why, you ask, is this chapter after the chapter on design? Simple. Being introduced to basic design elements first will help you better analyze your specific situation. Don't do the design work until the initial site inspection has been conducted. Then, after the mantel has been designed, carry out a secondary site inspection. This is where you determine whether design intent and planned dimensions actually will work.

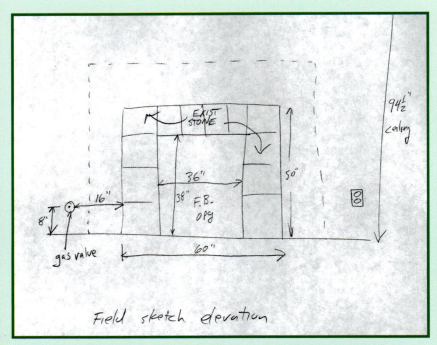

Field sketch elevation

31. Field sketch elevation shows existing fireplace conditions. Elevations show all vertical and horizontal dimensions of the fireplace wall.

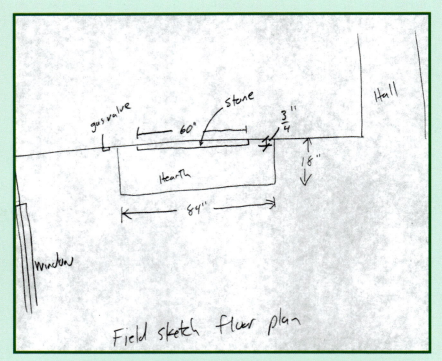

Field sketch floor plan

32. This field sketch plan shows elements of the room. Plan views will show the fireplace in relation to the rest of the room's elements.

Approach site inspection like a detective looking for clues. Your goal is to determine what the parameters of the mantel design are. For instance, you may be dreaming of a massive mantel with ultra wide 16-inch pilasters, only to discover the wall on one side of the firebox is only 10 inches wide where it meets the hallway passage. Or perhaps the firebox is situated only 16 inches from an inside corner, which wouldn't leave you enough space for both non-combustible material and a pilaster. Ideas and dreams (conceptualization) are where we start in every project. More often than not they elevate our ideals into the clouds. Reality (cost, skill level, available tooling, existing site conditions, etc.) has a way of bringing us out of the clouds and determining what will actually take place. Even if you have an unlimited budget and are a highly skilled woodworker, site conditions will ultimately dictate what you can do. Having said this, carefully review the site not only for dimensions, but for details that affect how to build and install the mantel.

The first thing I ask during every site inspection is: What type of mantel would look good here? Is the overall design going to work with the existing conditions? Perhaps you envision a full wrap mantelpiece with pilasters, frieze, and cornice to go around your new wood stove insert. The disappointment sets in when you discover that the attached metal shroud on the stove cannot be modified and leaves no room for pilasters on the sides. Now you may be forced to have only a shelf on corbels. Or, perhaps you visited a friend's house and fell in love with their mantel that incorporated cabinetry on either side of the fireplace. Knowing you had similar conditions in your house, you started to plan on putting a new stereo in the mantel cabinetry. Upon site review your dimensions revealed that in order to house a stereo in the adjoining cabinetry, you would have to sacrifice the raised panel pilasters for skinny flat ones. Dimensions are fixed, they cannot be changed unless you plan on changing the wall configuration. On some projects, that is the only alternative. For the sake of our discussion, we will consider the walls a static force to be reckoned with.

Now draw a simple sketch of the existing site conditions. It is from this sketch that you will draw your working shop drawings. These are drawn to scale and show all pertinent information, including dimensions, overall design, and notes that tell you how to both fabricate and install the mantel. Keep this in mind and get all the information necessary for your sketch. Include the three basic views of elevation, floor plan, and section. A field sketch can be crude; you'll be able to clean it up when you make your working (or shop) drawings. Just be certain everything is decipherable. The elevation is a front view showing what the wall of the fireplace looks like (Figure 31). A floor plan is a view looking down at the room (Figure 32). A section is a vertical view or "slice" that looks through the mantel (Figure 33). The elevation shows all the

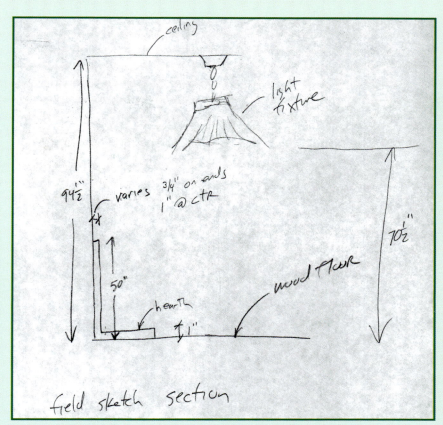

33. A field sketch's wall section show further details. This drawing helps the builder determine how each of the mantel's parts relate to each other. Both vertical sections (as shown) and horizontal (or plan view) sections are helpful tools.

heights and widths—the vertical plane. This includes walls, firebox, ceiling, raised hearths, existing stone surround, gas shut-off location, etc. The horizontal plane, or floor plan, will show the depth of the mantel as well as objects in front of the mantel and the surrounding wall configurations. The sectional drawing shows projection from the wall, greater detail, and the relationship of parts to each other.

It is critical to have all three views because two-dimensional drawings only show two points of view. This is not sufficient for a three-dimensional object being fabricated for a three-dimensional

34. When measuring the stone surround, be sure to dimension both top and bottom locations. Discovered discrepancies may alter the way you fabricate the object. In addition to the obvious dimensions, double-check for gas valve and electrical outlet locations.

35. Knowing if a wall is plumb (perfectly vertical) is critical before fabrication. A 4-foot level should be adequate for most applications.

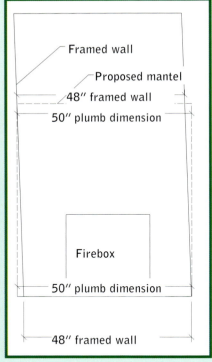

Framed wall

Proposed mantel

48" framed wall

50" plumb dimension

Firebox

50" plumb dimension

48" framed wall

36. Always check a wall for plumb to eliminate installation surprises. A wall may measure the same distance on top and bottom but if it is not plumb, the mantel will have to be made larger.

room. For instance, elevations show the two dimensions of the x (horizontal or width) axis and y (vertical or height) axis. Plan views show the two dimensions of the x axis and z (depth) axis. Vertical sections show the y and z axis. All three dimensional views are critical for arming yourself with enough information to lay the job out.

Get every dimension you can think of. Dimensions to look for are: firebox opening, stone slip, wall width, ceiling height, projection of brick off the wall, wall offsets or alcoves, location of windows and doors, hearth dimensions, fireplace insert dimensions, electrical outlets, gas shut-off valves, locations of existing stone, carpet, and wood flooring transitions, existing furniture layout, and any other pertinent detail you deem important (Figure 33). More is better. Just make the drawing big enough to house all the dimensions you place there. I've learned to make my sketches as clear as possible. I will often take field dimensions months before shop drawings and fabrication begins. If your drawing is sloppy, this can lead to errors. That is one of the reasons why I always make a second site visit prior to fabrication.

Site inspection requires its own unique toolbox. Items to consider including are: tape measure, T-bevel square, framing square, 4-foot level, profile duplicator, stud finder, calculator, templating material, story pole, moulding profile samples, painter's blue masking tape, and the obvious paper and pencil (Figure 30, page 30). These tools will help you transfer the information you gather to the workbench. Make sure you have a good tape measure from which to gather dimensions. The 25- or 30-foot models work well because they have a stout one-inch wide blade that deflects less over longer distances. Don't rely on the tape measure's end hook for precise measurements. "Burn" an inch by placing the one-inch line on the starting point and subtracting one inch from the end point. When possible, always measure both the top and bottom of a wall. Differing dimensions can reveal potential problems to avoid in fabrication. A T-bevel square allows you to transfer both acute and obtuse angles; this is especially helpful for corner fireplaces. Once an angle is measured, transfer it to a piece of wood or cardboard, labeling its location. A framing square, with its 24-inch leg, helps you determine how square inside and outside wall corners are. The smallest level you'll need is 4 feet.

Dimensioning walls is not enough; be sure to check for plumb (Figure 35). A wall can have the same dimension on both the top and bottom, but if it is not plumb you'll need to increase the width of the mantel to make up the difference (Figure 36). Checking for plumb can be the difference between a mantel fitting correctly or ending up back at the shop.

You can also use the level as a straight edge to determine how flat the wall is. If there is a big bow in the center of the fireplace, now is the time to find out. Another good tool to have is a profile duplicator (Figure 37). These may not be

37. Profile duplicators work by moving the individual segments into a mouldings profile. Then, transferring the shape on a template or piece of wood, the matching profile can be duplicated.

38. I transfer the shape onto a piece of cardboard first. Holding the cut cardboard up to the original helps determine any fine-tuning requirements.

39. Much like a doctor using a stethoscope to diagnose what he cannot see, I like to find framing locations in a wall during the site inspection. This may determine how the mantel gets fabricated, since attachment to the wall is a critical concern.

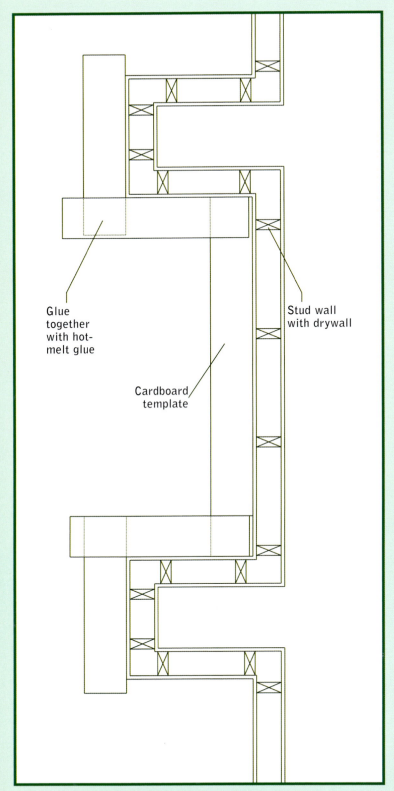

Glue
together
with hot-
melt glue

Stud wall
with drywall

Cardboard
template

40. Using a cardboard template is an easy way to determine the exact angles and conditions of a wall opening. Simply cut the material to fit the wall contour, and glue together with hot-melt glue.

available at the local hardware store, but most specialty stores or mail order catalogs carry them. These tools are used primarily to help duplicate a moulding profile, shape, relief, or other detail when you can't remove a sample piece of moulding. If you have an older home with unique mouldings that you want to duplicate, the profiler makes a good working moulding rendition. Once you have laid out the profile, transfer it to a piece of wood for safe keeping. Then copy it to paper or cardboard for your template. Carefully cut it out with a sharp knife and hold it up to the moulding (Figure 38). If the template does not fit perfectly, you can fine tune it to the actual profile.

The stud finder helps you locate framing members behind wallboard (Figure 39). There are different models available, but all work about the same. I have yet to find a stud finder that gives me consistent results, but they are still handy to have. If you don't want to invest in one, lightly knock across the wall with a hammer or your fist. You will hear a distinct hollow sound as the knocking passes over the wall cavity. The pitch changes as you come up to a stud. Also, I always have a calculator on hand because it helps me do quick, accurate math. You can quickly double-check consecutive wall dimensions and the feasibility of possible design solutions based on dimensions.

Another good tool to arm yourself with is a template. Actually, you arm yourself with the templating material and make a template while on site. A template is a pattern made of existing site conditions. Templating allows you to recreate the whole wall and take it back to your shop. The template provides all dimensions and angles. Write the dimensions down on the template, in addition to your sketch, at each corresponding location.

There are several different ways to make a template. The three I use the most are the cardboard template, the wood batten, and the plastic laminate. Each have advantages. Cardboard templating is the simplest (Figure 40). You'll need flat cardboard strips, a sharp knife, and a hot-melt glue gun. Cut the cardboard into strips 4 to 6 inches wide. While on the site, cut the strips about 1 inch less for inside corners and 6 inches more for outside corners. Use hot-melt glue to join the cardboard together. Start at inside corners first and work your way around the wall, holding each glue joint tight to the wall until hardened (usually a few seconds). Make any important notations right on the template. Large bows in the wall can easily be cut to fit. Smaller wall imperfections can just be noted on the template.

The wood batten method involves cutting 1/4-inch plywood strips about 2 inches wide by 8 feet long. The procedure for making this template is the same technique as the cardboard method. For a better connection at the joints, you may opt to use yellow glue and brads instead of hot-melt glue. I use this templating method when I need a good rigid template. The plastic laminate method uses a large cardboard piece as its base, com-

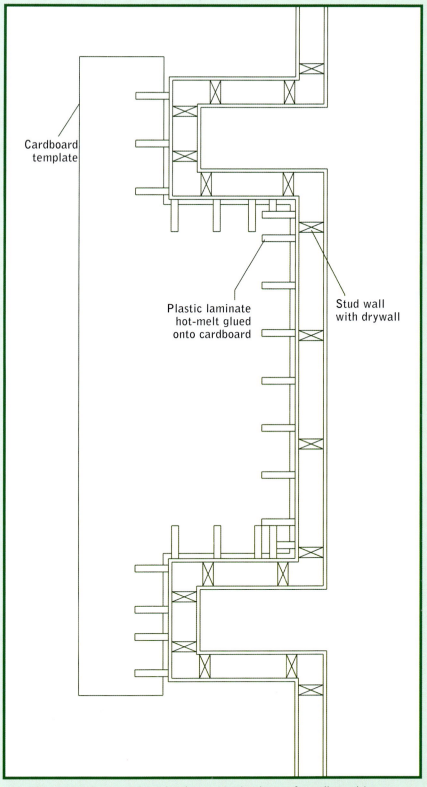

41. Plastic laminate strips glued to a single sheet of cardboard is a quick way to make an excellent template. The idea behind this method is to provide wall locations every 4 inches or so. A line is drawn from each laminate location much like connecting-the-dots.

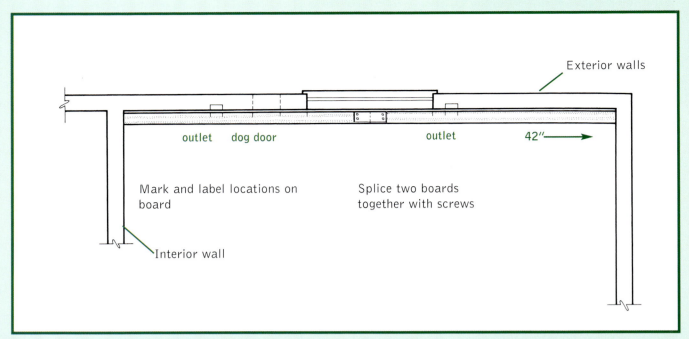

Exterior walls

outlet   dog door   outlet   42″ →

Mark and label locations on
board

Splice two boards
together with screws

Interior wall

42. A story pole records all of a wall's elements (outlets, windows, etc.) including dimensions, onto a single or screwed together piece of wood. Some prefer to use this method over making a sketch.

bined with 1-inch x 4-inch plastic laminate pieces. Cut the cardboard one to two inches smaller than the opening. Hot-melt glue the plastic laminate pieces to the cardboard (Figure 41). Space the strips about every 4 inches or wherever you feel you need one.

Which templating process should you use? While cardboard is easier to work with and faster, it is also the least accurate. The 1/4-inch boards are stiffer and hold tighter to the wall, resulting in more accuracy. In addition, the added stiffness means it will be less prone to changing shape. Plastic laminate is good for fine detail since you can place the contact points wherever you want them. For most mantel work, I prefer cardboard because of its simplicity. If I am constructing a more complex project where the margin of error is great, I opt for another method that will give me the

detail and accuracy I need. Remember to include all the dimensions on the sketch as well as the template.

A close cousin to the template is the story pole. Many cabinet-makers swear by these, insisting it is the only accurate way to measure a job. Knowing that dimensions going from a tape measure to a piece of paper can result in mistakes, many rely on the story pole for consistency. Start with a board measuring at least 3/4 inch x 1-1/2 inch. Typically I use 8-foot lengths. If the wall is longer than eight feet, the boards get screwed together and indexed once reassembled in the shop. To create a story pole, place the board against the wall. Transfer all dimensions, wall changes, windows, stone locations, etc. right where they happen (Figure 42). Story poles are great tools when used together with a job site

sketch. Story poles rarely lie because they rely on the accuracy of placing a pencil mark right where a detail is, rather than a tape measure and sketch. An old-timers' favorite, some of my mentors relied on them exclusively. They felt it was the best way to bring the job site into the shop to confirm their dimensions. Mantels are fairly simple and straightforward; most require only a good sketch. If, however, your situation is complex, I highly recommend the story pole.

If possible, bring some moulding samples to the site. There is no better way to get a feel for the use of mouldings than to have pieces to play with. Along those same lines, masking tape can be put on the wall where you plan to have the mantel. Make sure you use a good quality, nonstick type of tape such as blue painter's tape. The cheaper varieties of masking tape can pull paint off the wall and, if left on too long, will leave a residue of glue on the wall surface that is hard to clean off. Although not as sophisticated as setting up a cardboard pattern (as discussed in Chapter 2), taping up the mantel outline will give you a good sense of scale. And it's a very easy way to play with details.

The site review is not yet complete. After you make a sketch with dimensions, story pole, or necessary templates, you have a few other items that need to be researched. How and where are you going to fasten the mantel to the wall? Now is the time to figure that out. You don't want to design something that cannot be safely attached. For instance, noncombustible materials cannot be attached directly to the firebox masonry. They can, however, be safely attached to the brick veneer. If you are uncertain what conditions and materials you have, contact your local building official for assistance. Use the stud finder to determine where framing materials are. Think about how the attachment of the mantel will affect fabrication. Will it require adding extra blocking to the mantelpiece? I've had jobs where I discovered that by adding the necessary blocking in the wall before fabrication, I was able to cover up the wall damage with the finished millwork. How much, if any, of the brick or stone work will be covered? What is access to the job like? Will that full mantel surround fit through the narrow entry hall leading to the room where the mantel will reside? If you have any

doubts, make a mock-up to walk through the site. If this is a concern, I'll cut a board the depth and length of the mantel. Then, walking the board through the house can help determine problematic situations.

Does the complexity of the mantel and its installation suggest it should be painted on site instead of in the shop? Is there enough room for a pilaster around the gas shut-off valve when the key is inserted? Does the existing stone that you want to keep provide enough space around the opening so you won't violate the Uniform Building Codes (Chapter 2)? Are you planning on eventually changing your open fireplace design into a wood or gas insert? If so, how will that affect the mantel you have planned? Ask yourself as many questions as possible. Try to be thorough.

Make sure you dimension the overall room—not just the fireplace and items that are directly around the mantel. Include ceiling heights, overall room dimensions, door and window locations, and any other significant details. I reiterate this because in the design phase, these dimensions will be very helpful in determining how things fit together as a whole. Your mantel is going to become part of a room and part of the structure itself. It will not stand alone; it will interact with the architecture around it.

It is critical to make your shop drawings to scale. This doesn't have to be an elaborate drawing, but when drawn to scale it will help illustrate how the project will end up looking. Building a custom

Shop drawings

All phases of a project typically are not built from a single set of architectural drawings. On more complex jobs it is common to have a set of engineering plans as well as plans for all the structural elements. These drawings could be considered the master plans that shape the structure being built. Most fixtures and finished work will be found on the architectural drawings. Since these architectural drawings convey design intent only, it is up to the subcontractor to make his own set of drawings to show how his items will be built. These shop drawings are working drawings used to fabricate specific items. Every trade that builds prefabricated objects for a construction project uses shop drawings. This includes architectural woodwork (cabinetry, paneling, mouldings), sheetmetal (architectural, ductwork), steel work (structural beams), and lumber manufacturers (trusses, glu-lam beams), to name a few.

Even when building a project for yourself, a working set of drawings will help you in the following:

- 1. Design - Proportion, including elements in a room, function, etc.

- 2. Fabrication - Dimensioning, cutting materials, machining, determining assembly sequence, tooling needs, etc.

- 3. Conveying your ideas to others.

It's easy to understand the first two reasons for doing shop drawings because they appeal to your sense of logic. The last reason, conveying your idea to others, may not seem valid on a project you're building for yourself. That reasoning is incorrect. Although you may not be dealing with an architect who cradles his project like a baby or a picky designer who is drooling at the chance to tell you what to change, you need to have a visual representation of the project before you begin. One of the most important people you need to show the drawings to is yourself. Conveying design intent to the builder (you) is a key ingredient to convincing the builder to proceed with the project. If you don't feel right about the design, you'll struggle with the whole fabrication process.

43. Many people still prefer shop drawings done by hand to computer-aided drafting. The inexpensive set of tools you need would include a stable drawing board, T-square, mechanical pencils, triangles and assorted templates.

piece requires as much visualization as possible before cutting material and spending valuable time in the shop. For smaller jobs like this I usually use 1/2" = 1' in scale. With this scale, both the elevation and partial floor plan fit on an 8-1/2 x 11-inch sheet of paper. If details are necessary, try to use at least 1-1/2" = 1' scale. These are easily drawn by hand with an architect's scale and a straight edge. If you prefer using a computer, there are some good basic computer-assisted drafting (CAD) software programs available. I cannot overemphasize the importance of drawings. The temptation may be to forego the drawings, jump into the shop, and start the project. I suppose that's fine if the project is simple, or if you're really comfortable with design and how to fabricate. However, it has been my experience that disciplining yourself to draw the plan forces you to build the project on paper first. This greatly lessens the chance for mistakes and frustrating experiences during fabrication, even if you have repeatedly done this type of work. A well-planned project has a much greater chance of success than winging it by the seat of your pants.

GETTING STARTED

Making shop drawings can be simple. I'll describe the ideal, but a simpler approach may be more appropriate for your situation. A pad of paper and pencil may be all you need to get started. To be more technical, get a small drafting kit. Basic items needed to get you going would include (Figure 43):

- T-square - Used to draw straight horizontal lines.
- Triangles - Common ones are 45 degrees and 30/60 degrees. These are used to draw both the angle shown and a vertical 90-degree line.
- Mechanical pencil - Stock it with both 0.7mm (thicker lines) and 0.5mm lines (fine lines) and an assortment of soft and hard pencil leads
- Erasers - For the obvious mistakes
- Compass set -   Handy for drawing circles, arcs, and dividing lines.
- Architectural scale - Necessary for drawing objects to scale.
- French curves - Used for drawing irregular curves.
- Templates - Various useful templates might include lettering, shapes (circle, square), architectural symbols
- Drawing board - Small portable unit or an existing desktop will do.

With a little practice, anyone can make simple shop drawings. Because you'll be using drafting tools, the drawing experience will be structured. Don't totally eliminate creative expression, however. Being relaxed will help you achieve a good set of drawings.

If you are computer literate and prefer to do your drawings electronically, you're in luck. Many good CAD programs are available ranging from $50 to $500. If starting out, I recommend a basic program to get familiar with the process. With CAD software, you will be able to draw virtually anything. If you're used to drawing with pencil and paper, the biggest adjustment will be not being able to see the entire drawing at once: drawing on the computer limits your view to what the screen will

hold. If you plan to do much drawing, you'll find that CAD's strengths outweigh its weaknesses. Strengths include easy revisions and multiple or repetitive drawings—a tremendous time saver for the frequent user.

When the bulk of the design process has been conducted, shop drawings have been completed, and you are drawing near to the fabrication stage, your mind can better focus on dimensioning. Are your dimensions correct? Will the dimensions work with the existing conditions of hearth size, gas-valve locations, etc.? This is when you make the secondary site inspection tour. Armed with your shop drawings, preliminary dimensions and other pertinent design information, you are ready for the second review. Something happens between the first and second site visit. Much like a sandwich that has the meat in the middle, your design work on paper rests between the two site visits. In order to make it a palatable sandwich, you must double-check all your work. You will be amazed, either at how accurate you were the first time through, or at how many mistakes you made. Incorrect dimensions or object placement will readily jump out at you. That is what the design process does. From conceptualization during the initial site visit, through discovery as you actually design the mantel, finally you enter the stage of implementation where your project is realized.

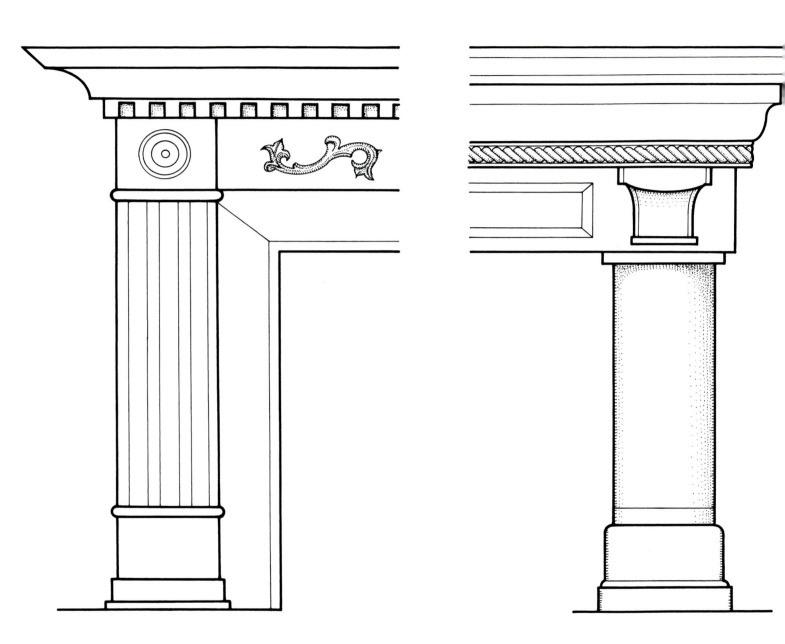

44. Mantels can use a wide variety of mouldings. Simple or complex, their use is limited only by your imagination.

CHAPTER 4

Materials for Mantels

MUCH OF THE FUN IN BUILDING A mantel comes from the wide range of products available. Depending on your skill level or participation in the project, you can purchase raw materials and build everything, or buy component parts that you assemble into your own design. For instance, plaster corbels could be purchased for the shelf supports, requiring only a simple wood cornice shelf to complete the project. Or, you could purchase a highly decorative complete mantel kit fabricated in plaster or cast stone. This alternative requires only installation and painting. One of the most common approaches is to build the basic mantel surround and buy all the applied mouldings. The only real drawback to component assembly is the dimension restraints. Although they can be used in many situations, they have restrictions. If you are looking for a truly custom fit and design, you may need to fabricate all component parts. There is nothing to be ashamed of if you choose to build a mantel with components. Virtually every consumable product we purchase is built this way. If you have any part of the design, fabrication, and installation of the mantel, it will still be your project, even if your participation comes just from reading this book.

Select materials that will work with your design. Choosing natural wood can be complex since the array of wood selection is so great. Paint-grade mantels also have many options, and materials should be carefully selected. If you are daring, have the proper space, budget, and desire for a full stone mantel surround, I salute you. Although beyond the scope of this book, they are worth mentioning. Fabricating a stone mantel is not for the do-it-yourselfer or faint-hearted.

There are two basic material choices for wood mantels: natural and paint grade, or any combination of the two. Natural wood is defined as any species of wood incorporating a stained or clear finish. Chapter 7 discusses the fabrication for a simple, natural wood mantel. Paint grade is just as the name implies: something that will receive an opaque finish. Construction techniques for a paint grade mantel are discussed in Chapter 8. Both choices can incorporate solid wood, veneers, and composites.

Solid wood is best defined as lumber sawn from a tree in one inch and thicker planks. This is what we will refer to as wood thickness. Two classes of wood are softwoods and hardwoods. Softwood trees are those known as coniferous or cone-bearing, such as fir, pine, cedar, and hemlock. Leaf-bearing trees such as oak, maple, cherry, walnut, etc. are classified as hardwoods. Common lumber yards sell softwood and building materials only. Some, however, do carry a limited assortment of hardwood, mouldings, and paint-grade materials. You usually need to find a specialty lumber yard that carries a good hardwood selection. Softwood, solid wood, is sold as dimensioned lumber. That means it has been milled to a specific thickness, width and length. Softwood lumber is sold by the linear foot. The dimension it is sold as is a nominal –in name only–dimension. In other words, a common 2 x 4 is actually 1-1/2 inches x 3-1/2 inches. This is because the mill rough-saws it to 2 inches x 4 inches. Then it is machined down to the finished nominal dimension of 1-1/2 inches x 3-1/2 inches.

Hardwood lumber is typically sold by the board foot because it comes in random widths and lengths. One board foot is based on 1 inch of thickness by 12 inches of width and 12 inches of length. The formula for figuring this out (with all dimensions in inches) is thickness x width x length divided by 144. Hardwood lumber is also milled into dimensional lumber and sold by the linear foot. Purchasing it this way is considerably more expensive. Solid woods are typically used in one form or another on mantels. Mouldings are commonly made of solid wood. In addition, some mantel parts work best with solid wood rather than composites. The only drawback to their use is the amount of prep work that must be done to achieve a finished product. When the mantel design calls for large panels, veneer is a better choice because of labor savings and greater stability (refer to Chapter 8 on fabricating for seasonal changes).

Veneers are thin slices of wood bonded onto a substrate. The substrate is typically a composite panel product that offers greater stability and in some cases more strength than solid wood. Plywood is such a material. The surface veneers are thin, usually 1/28 thick on commercially purchased products. Although that is a very thin piece of wood, it is more than adequate when used in the right application and when care is taken. Since plywood is available in sheet sizes larger than solid wood, it offers many advantages. First, there is less preparation required for panel assembly. Pieces won't have to be glued together to make up wide panels. This saves additional time since planing is eliminated and sanding is minimized. Plywood is also very stable. It does not move as much as solid wood during seasonal humidity changes. The disadvantage is that since it is a composite material, the edges must be covered.

Plywood is available with different types of cores. The veneer core has cross banding of several plies or veneers (Figure 45). The grain of each different layer or ply runs perpendicular to the adjoining ply. Veneer cores are the most common, offer the greatest strength, are the lightest in weight, and the most expensive. Being the strongest and most expensive does not necessarily mean they are the best choice for every application. Since the plies under the face veneer have grain patterns and possible defects, one must be aware that these can telegraph through and be seen in the face veneer.

Particleboard and **medium-density fiberboard** (MDF) cores are probably the most maligned of

45. Composite lumber or panel products include: (top) medium density fiberboard; (2nd from top) particleboard; (3rd from top) veneer core plywood; (bottom) Classic core.

all panel products. Almost everyone associates particleboard with cheap construction. Although these are the least expensive to purchase, they offer the best core for the veneer. Since the core is the same material throughout, the veneer shows only the beauty of its own characteristics. Particleboard and MDF cores are in the same weight, price, and strength class. MDF is a smoother core and advantageous if the core needs to be routed (Figure 45-top). Particleboard, on the other hand, has better ability to hold a screw (Figure 45, previous page). The newest core material available is Classic or Pro Core–each manufacturer calls it something different (Figure 45-bottom). Classic Core has the light weight of a veneer ply, which is sandwiched in the middle of either a particleboard or MDF substrate. With the better characteristics of MDF or particleboard directly under the surface veneer and the inclusion of veneer plies, you get the best of a veneer core's strength and an MDF core's lack of defects. As suspected, it is priced in the middle of the two products as well. It's a good choice for most projects.

If your mantel design calls for natural wood, your first decision will be the species. If you are going to match elements in the house, your choice may simply be narrowed down by the wood already there. However, if the wood species is limited only by what you desire, your options can seem endless. Wood choices are vast and selecting the right one can be a daunting task. One obstacle will be the availability of the material. While there may not be many choices where you live, most woods can be acquired through mail order. The determining factor will be how much of the work you want to do yourself and how much money you want to invest in the project. For instance, if you choose an exotic wood for your mantel, the most cost-effective method is to use veneer for the mantel body. Additionally, some exotic species are only going to be readily available as veneers. Exotic solid lumber prices can be prohibitive because the wood is scarce. For panels, hardwood plywood is generally only stocked in domestic and a few commonly used exotic species. If specialized exotics are used, you'll have to veneer it yourself. In addition, if mouldings are a key component in the design, their availability will greatly influence your species selection. Unless, of course, you have the ability to shape your own.

The most common stock mouldings in my area are red oak, maple, Philippine mahogany, and cherry. Along with that, the profile selections are limited and finding the stock moulding you want may not be possible. Any other species would require a special moulding run. If you elect to make your own mouldings, or have them custom run, the selection of species is then made solely upon your creative desires.

If the plan is to have the mantel act as an accent, or stand-alone piece, a different approach will need to be taken in picking out the species. There is nothing that says you have to use the same species throughout the mantel. In fact, if planned properly, you can even mix natural wood and painted. If you do mix species, make the combinations compatible. Understanding the characteristics of wood and how it makes a piece look, is key in deciding what species to pick. Open-grain woods such as oak, walnut, ash, and mahogany create a textured look, even when the grain is filled. Closed-grain hardwoods like maple, cherry, and birch lend themselves to a contemporary, smooth appearance. Softwoods like pine, fir, and cedar give a room a rustic feeling and should be used accordingly. Remember this about design (Chapter 2): when selecting a species, use rules as a guideline only. Sometimes when rules are broken we achieve fantastic results. Go with your best instinct. I'll take the time to remind you that the design mindset runs through the whole process of building a mantel, like a thread running through a garment. Species selection needs to be considered in your design.

Both natural wood and painted mantels will usually be fabricated from a combination of solid wood and veneers. The solid wood is used in the frame, mouldings, and miscellaneous trims. Veneers comprise the box or larger panels in the piece. Your project could also be all solid wood; it just depends on the design. For instance: if the panels are raised, or your design dictates the use of solid wood, or if you simply prefer to work with it, then solid wood could be the

only material implemented. In Chapter 7, I discuss the construction of a solid wood mantel. More complex mantels, however, usually incorporate both solid wood and veneers.

Paint-grade mantels offer more flexibility in material choices. Because the material receives an opaque finish, different wood materials can easily be mixed. The main thing to consider in wood choice is grain. If a smooth finish is what you want, don't use open-grained woods like oak or mahogany. You probably wouldn't anyway, since they cost more. Also, don't be tempted to use up open-grained wood scraps lying around from another project. Other things to avoid are heavy coarse grain and knots. Just because it's getting painted doesn't mean it will cover up easily. You want to have a smooth substrate for the finish to rest on. Knots and other defects often telegraph through, even with extensive preparation. Softwoods like fir, pine, and hemlock can be painted with good results if care is taken in preparing the material. The broad grain in fir and hemlock, and the knots in pine have discouraged me from consistently using these species for paint-grade work. In addition, the clear grades of these materials (i.e., vertical-grain fir and clear pine), typically cost more than some hardwoods. Therefore, my hardwoods of choice are poplar, maple, and alder. I'll also use cherry and birch (paint-compatible species) if I have some scrap wood I want to use up. Poplar is the least expen-

46. Medium density overlay, or MDO, is another excellent paint-grade panel that offers superior strength. It gets its strength because it is manufactured with several layers or plies of wood veneer. It paints well because it is overlaid with a paper that has no grain or knots.

47. Manufactured panel products are popular because they provide the fabricator with large panels requiring no gluing and minimal sanding. However, the core must either be concealed in a frame or covered with edge banding. Square, contemporary looking edges can be achieved by veneering (top). When shaping a profile, solid wood edge banding must be applied (bottom).

sive of the three and is easily machined and sanded. Its only drawback is that it is somewhat soft and damages easier upon impact. Alder has the same basic characteristics as poplar, it just costs a little more. Maple is a good-closed grain wood and is much harder. Its only drawbacks are cost and machineability. It tends to tear-out more when profiling edges. If I have a project with moving parts like doors, or if a piece will be subject to great abuse, I choose maple because it is very durable.

Whenever I can substitute a composite product for solid lumber I do; it usually saves both time and money. When incorporating composite materials in a paint-grade project, two choices avail themselves: veneer plywood and medium density fiberboard (MDF). Maple and birch plywood, as well as medium density overlay (MDO) are excellent choices for paint grade work. MDO is also known as signboard (Figure 46). It is a veneered plywood product with a thin, paintable face bonded to the outer plies. The best advantage to MDO is that the paper face has no grain to cover up with paint. So long as the panels are inset into a frame they work great. Since plywood products have an exposed core that cannot be machined or painted, it must be banded. Typically, it is banded with solid wood that it creates a decorative edge (Figure 47). However, no matter how well this edge is attached, the joint will usually be visible after painting. Painting accentuates defects and joints; it does not cover them up. You could also veneer the edge, but then would be limited to having a square edge (Figure 47-top). Veneered edges are not very durable and are prone to damage, therefore, they are not a viable solution in mantel projects. In addition, veneered plywood products typically cost more. Another option is MDF.

Do not confuse MDF with particleboard. Medium density fiberboard is manufactured from long-fibered softwood chips, shavings and sawdust. Uniform density allows for detailed edge and face machining without splintering or chipping. This is a significant advantage over the machining of hardwood lumber. The face is silky smooth and lends itself well to painting. It is available in different forms: exterior grade for outside use; formaldehyde free, which is manufactured without formaldehyde binders; ultra light, which is much lighter in weight; and the standard interior grade. There are also different qualities of interior grade MDF. Specify the superior grade; it machines and paints better. Each manufacturer's product is slightly different. Talk to your local supplier to determine which interior product is best.

What are the advantages of using MDF over veneer plywood? First, it costs less than veneer plywood. Second, you can rout the edges, eliminating the need for edgebanding. Third, it's a widely accepted material for use in the moulding industry and has a proven track record. It works great for mantel cornices because shelves are wide and have some type of profiled edge. With MDF, this can all be accomplished without introducing another material (such as edgebanding). With plywood, you would have to add edgebanding. There are two disadvantages to using MDF worth noting. One is that MDF is considerably heavier than veneer plywood. The other is the dust generated when machining can be hazardous. If you are able to purchase formaldehyde-free MDF, the dust is not as dangerous. In either case, be sure to wear a dust mask.

In addition to the available wood mouldings, we can now add plastics to our palette of choices when constructing painted mantels. This would include foam and polyurethane products like polystyrene. Designed for use in paint-grade products, foam mouldings provide a wide range of design possibilities. These extruded styrene mouldings are lightweight, easy to work with, and economical. Not to be ignored by the wood purist, the level of detail is much greater and offers many more options than real wood. They are a great alternative if you don't like to nail wood or deal with splinters; the material is often too soft for nails to grab. Many of the products require glue, with a few nails tacked in to hold it in place while the adhesive sets up.

Pre-cast plaster and gypsum parts can also be acquired. If you're looking for a set of decorative corbels that have an intricately carved look, a pre-cast product would be an excellent choice. The time and cost to produce true wood carvings would be prohibitive to most. So long as the mantel is being painted, these would be the way to go.

Stone mantels have a feeling of authority and elegance. Because of their cost, stone mantels are strictly a high-end product. Historically they were built only for the elite who could afford them. Even though they were later found in more common homes, they have always been expensive. When seen in large rooms with high ceilings, they command a second look. In fact, they dictate the feeling of a room, to an even greater extent in a small room. Stone is a dominant material. Even marble and limestone, softer in appearance than granite, still exudes strength. Unlike wood, which can be either subtle or loud, stone, in large amounts, is always loud. Although beautiful in appearance, it generates a cold feeling. This is not necessarily a bad thing, just something to consider.

If you are thinking along these lines, find a stone mantel to look at before committing to the purchase. Most fabricators will gladly give you a referral list. It's a large investment and will give the room a specific motif. Design possibilities are increased since stone is non-combustible (Chapter 2). Unless you have the skill and tooling to work with stone, you will have to hire someone. Stonework is a highly skilled craft and not suited for the do-it-yourselfer. Although beyond the scope of this book, stone mantels are a viable consideration. Many of the same design principles will apply. Since most contemporary mantels are made of wood, the tendency is to ignore stone altogether. However, if you study stone mantel characteristics, you may find ideas to incorporate into your wood mantel, either through the use of stone itself or its overall appearance.

If you like the stone look but don't have the budget for stone, there are a couple of less expensive options to consider. These include cast stone, cultured marble and granite, and solid-surface materials like Corian. Of the three options, cast stone mantel surrounds share the closest characteristic of solid stone. It's a very durable product that has been used for many years. Cast stone is composed of silica sand and fine aggregates mixed together with bonding and hardening agents. Cultured marble and granite go through a similar manufacturing process, yet have a more artificial appearance. Solid-surface materials are available in many stone patterns and like wood, can be fabricated with great details.

Another disguised solid stone option would be to consider painting. There are techniques and paint products available that simulate stone. Many are "off-the-shelf" varieties that are fairly easy to use. Check with your paint supplier. Stone can also be introduced independently into the mantel shelf, hearth, and slips as a way of adding aggregate without significantly increasing the cost.

MOULDINGS

Mouldings and decorative appliqués are what give a mantel its distinctiveness (Figure 48). Even if these are not available locally, most can be acquired through mail order. Mouldings are described as anything formed by, or in, a mold, which is to make into a certain shape, to fit the contours of, to form according to some pattern, to modify the shape or character of, to decorate with mouldings. How perfectly this describes the mantel building process. That is what making a mantel is: decorating with mouldings. Described below are various common mouldings. It's not a complete list, which would be exhaustive, but a starting point. Available in wood and plastics, determine your choice based on availability, cost, and design.

CROWN

Crown moulding is typically used at the transition of wall and ceiling. Because it spans a vertical and horizontal surface, it becomes an ideal choice for use under mantel shelves and cornices. Crown can be used alone (Figure 49) or in combination with another moulding to form a built-up system (Figure 50).

CROWN WITH INTEGRATED ROPE OR DENTIL

This is a specialty crown that incorporates more detail in its design (Figure 51). Depending on where you buy this type of moulding, it may be a one-piece crown or, the trim piece (rope, dentil, etc.) may be separate. If separate, the location of the trim piece on

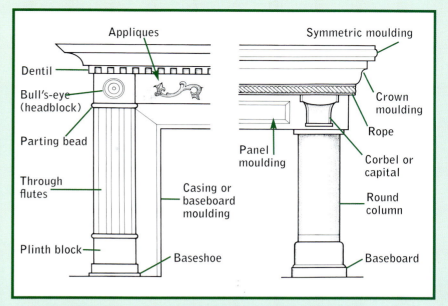

48. Mantels can use a wide variety of mouldings. Simple or complex, their use is limited only by your imagination. A larger version of this drawing apears on page 42.

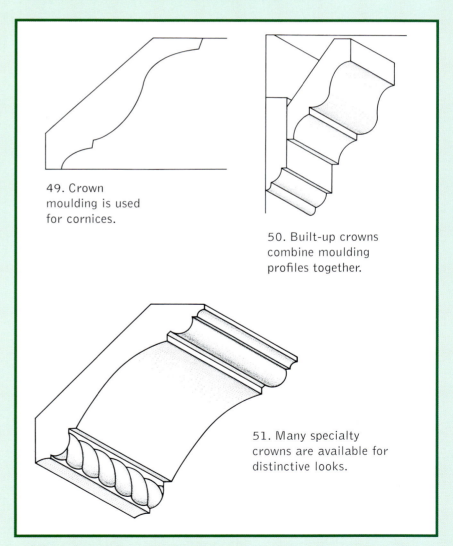

49. Crown moulding is used for cornices.

50. Built-up crowns combine moulding profiles together.

51. Many specialty crowns are available for distinctive looks.

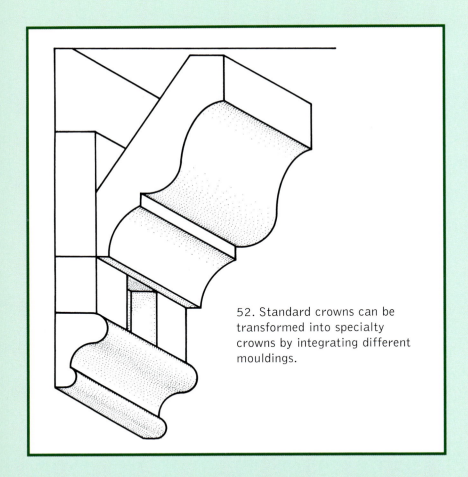

52. Standard crowns can be transformed into specialty crowns by integrating different mouldings.

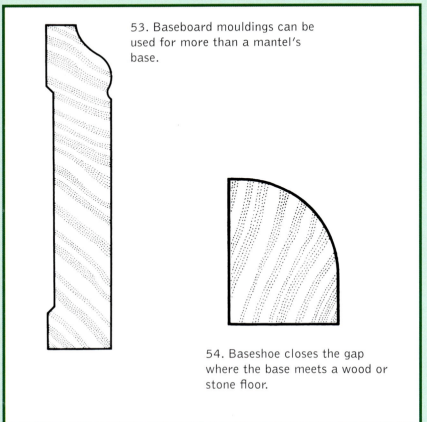

53. Baseboard mouldings can be used for more than a mantel's base.

54. Baseshoe closes the gap where the base meets a wood or stone floor.

the crown moulding will be flat so the flat back of the trim piece is easily attached. This does require extra fitting but usually is a cost-savings. In addition, you can mix species to create an accent. The mouldings with this trim integrated can be costly. If the mantel is receiving a painted finish, consider a foam crown; the integrated detail is not as costly as it is in wood. You can also achieve an integrated look by using a standard crown utilizing the built-up system (Figure 52).

BASEBOARD

Baseboard is one of the most common mouldings available. Baseboard can either be simple square stock or more decorative (Figure 53). One thing all baseboard has in common: it needs to have a flat back and bottom. Used at the base of a mantel's pilasters, it gives a sense of stability. Modern day construction practice has diminished the quality of the baseboard's significance. Usually 1-1/2 inches to 2-1/4 inches wide, today's baseboard is much smaller than its predecessors. When it comes to using baseboard on a mantel, think big. Erase the notion of the small base. Mantels need a tall base to stabilize their overall appearance. Since you need such a small amount of baseboard, relatively speaking, be generous in your selection.

BASESHOE

Typical baseshoe measures 1/2 inch x 3/4 inch h (Figure 54). Used at the bottom of baseboard to close the gap between the baseboard and wood flooring, baseshoe can add extra detail to your mantel. Any moulding with a flat back and bottom can be used as baseshoe.

CASING

Casing is typically associated with framing windows and door openings (Figure 55). Flat on the back and usually flat on one edge to accept baseboard that abutts it, casing can be used on mantels either as a base or applied moulding. Casing is readily available and can easily be modified by cutting off certain details. When using casing as an applied moulding, considerations must be made. Because of the one flat edge, the transition from the flat face of the box to the abrupt edge of the moulding creates too great a rise. Therefore, if using casing as an applied moulding, use it in conjunction with a panel. In this application it would be better to use a panel moulding.

PANEL MOULDINGS

Panel moulding is typically used to wrap a panel's edge (Figure 56). There will be two flat sides: one against the panel, the other against the wall. The exposed portion is profiled to provide a decorative and softened edge to a panel. The panel fills in the void created by the applied moulding. Studying the drawings reveals how to mate panel mouldings with a panel to create different effects. The first drawing shows a quirk, or small reveal, in the moulding where it meets the panel (Figure 57). This allows the moulding and panel to be flush to each other. Figure 58 is a detail for making the panel proj-

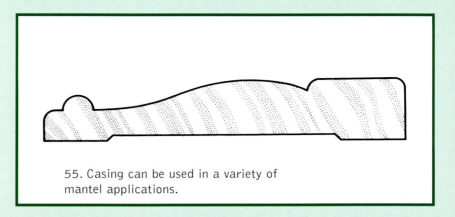

55. Casing can be used in a variety of mantel applications.

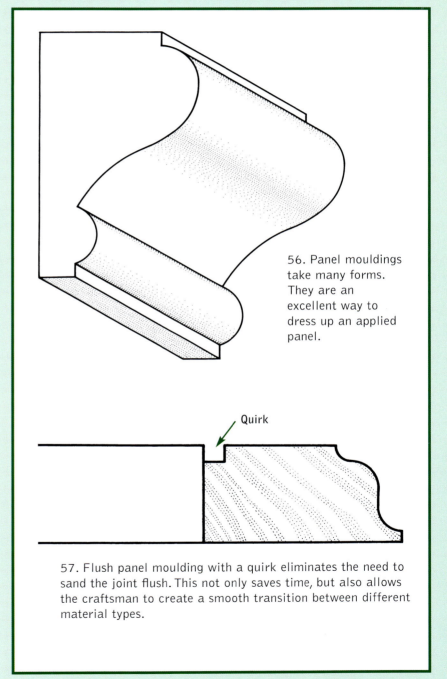

56. Panel mouldings take many forms. They are an excellent way to dress up an applied panel.

Quirk

57. Flush panel moulding with a quirk eliminates the need to sand the joint flush. This not only saves time, but also allows the craftsman to create a smooth transition between different material types.

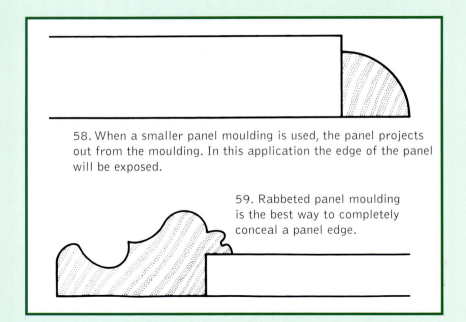

58. When a smaller panel moulding is used, the panel projects out from the moulding. In this application the edge of the panel will be exposed.

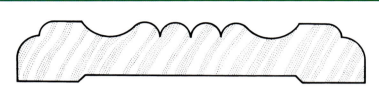

59. Rabbeted panel moulding is the best way to completely conceal a panel edge.

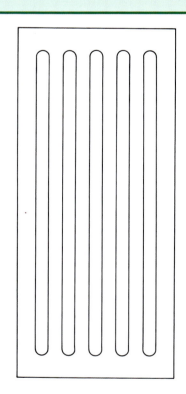

60. Symmetric mouldings have identical profiles on both edges and lend themselves well to pilasters.

61. Stopped flutes are an excellent choice for a rich-looking plinth. Stopped flutes must be custom-made to specified lengths.

ect out farther than the moulding. By stepping the moulding down from the panel edge, you not only raise the panel but you eliminate any inconsistencies between the two materials. The moulding can also stand proud of the panel as shown in Figure 59). The main thing to consider here is not to raise it too high. Note where the moulding rises above the panel it begins its shaped profile. If this area is flat or left too high, your eye will "hiccup" on the detail as it scans the profile, much like hitting a speed bump on the road. Or, the panel moulding can be used by itself as a picture frame detail with no inside panel.

SYMMETRIC MOULDINGS

Symmetric mouldings, as the name implies, have an identical or mirror pattern on both sides of the moulding (Figure 60). These are the mouldings of choice for applied mouldings, or even for entire pilasters. Since the profile is on both edges, you achieve a subtle transition from the box as your eye rolls over the moulding, unlike what would happen if you used casing in a similar application.

Beaded and fluted mouldings fall in the symmetric category. As an example: if you are not set up to make your own stopped flute pilaster, off-the-shelf fluted mouldings can be used. A stopped flute (Figure 61) must be custom-made since the length of the flute will always vary. Since they are more challenging to machine, you may not be up for the task. If that is the case, you can purchase through flutes (Figure 62) and beaded mouldings (Figure 63) already milled. Through flutes, as is the case for all purchased mouldings, have a profile running through the entire length of the board. To accommodate the starting and stopping of the profile, incorporate another moulding. Plinth blocks, head blocks (which would include rosettes and bull's-eyes), and parting beads, or any combination of these will accomplish this.

PLINTH BLOCKS

Plinth blocks (or base blocks) are used at the bottom of casings or symmetric mouldings (Figure 64). They allow the use of continuous mouldings by providing the necessary ending point. Because the casing or symmetrical moulding sits on top of the plinth block, it is more advantageous to have the block thicker than its complementary moulding (Figure 65). This creates a reveal for the upper moulding to rest on. If the two mouldings had the same thickness dimension, this reveal would be lost, resulting in an awkward transition. Plinth blocks can be as simple as a four-sided square block, or have a more detailed profile. They can also serve as the only base for the mantel, a stopping point for the baseboard on the pilaster side, or merely a stopping point for the symmetrical moulding, much like parting beads (described below).

HEAD BLOCKS

The term head block refers to the combination of a bull's-eye and other moulding. This is just a way

62. Through-flutes can be bought off the shelf. They will require a parting bead of some type to complete.

63. Beaded mouldings are the opposite of flutes_ convex half-rounds as opposed to the flute's concave half-round. These are an excellent choice for distinctive pilaster treatment.

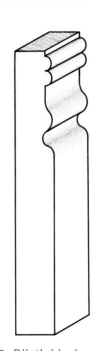

65. Plinth blocks are located at the bottom intersection of vertical and horizontal mouldings. By design, they provide the smooth transition between different profiles.

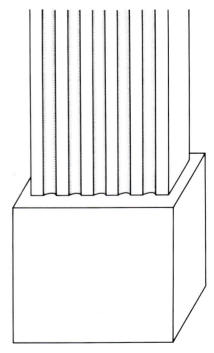

65. Plinth blocks are typically thicker than the moulding that joins them. Not only does this create interest through depth perception, but also ease in installation.

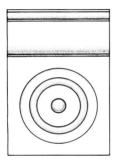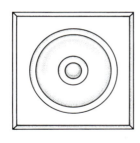

66. Head blocks are used at the top of a moulding transition much like plinth blocks are used at the bottom. They can be simple or ornate.

67. A bull's-eye is a form of head block that has a radiused imprint in its face.

68. If you can't find the bull's-eye or rosette you want, they can be made on a drill press. Shown is a rosette cutter housing with a replaceable cutter. Many patterns are available, or custom knives can be ground.

69. Rosettes are applied decorative mouldings.

70. Parting beads are used to separate two moulding profiles. The typical parting bead will have a bull-nosed edge. However, other profiles can be created.

of dressing up the block by making it more ornate, and you are limited only by your imagination. Head blocks provide the same function as plinth blocks, only they top the symmetrical moulding (Figure 66). Ornate or simple, these blocks allow creative use of mouldings. Head blocks can take many forms: bull's-eyes or corner blocks can either cap the vertical leg of a symmetrical moulding, or join both vertical legs and horizontal rails (Figure 67). Bull's-eyes usually have a radiused imprint in the block face, available in many profiles. You can make your own by investing in a simple cutter used in a standard drill press (Figure 68). Or the block face can be flat stock. Rosettes are bull's-eyes without the square part of the block (Figure 69). These plant-on mouldings can be applied anywhere. If used as a head block they have to be applied on a square piece of wood.

PARTING BEADS

Parting beads are the simplest way to divide continuous mouldings from other details. Used to stop or part the continuous moulding, parting beads draw little attention (Figure 70). As the name implies, these little mouldings usually have a radiused or bullnosed edge. To use them, set the beginning point of the radius beyond the moulding you are parting. Although commonly found with a bullnosed edge, you could be creative and rout a different profile to accommodate your design.

DENTIL TRIM

Dentil trim is usually found

below your mantel shelf. Composed of a series of small, closely spaced blocks, it gives the mantel a distinctive look. Many variations of the blocks are possible, but the most common would be a simple square block (Figure 71). Another type of dentil trim is the Greek variation (Figure 72). This is a more complex pattern because the wood is a continuous thread. More difficult to make, you may have better luck finding a supplier that carries it in stock. The Achilles heel of dentil trim comes in the finishing stage, particularly on a painted mantel. Great care must be taken to ensure even coating of front and side surfaces (refer to Chapter 10 on finishing).

DESIGNER OR DECORATIVE MOULDINGS

I classify these mouldings as custom, highly decorative type. Carved mouldings such as egg and dart (Figure 73) or appliqués (Figure 74) add a real hand-built look. Unless you are good at carving or have a lot of patience, I recommend purchasing these through mail order or specialty millwork shops. They are readily available but usually in limited species. If painting your mantel, this shouldn't be a problem. With a natural finish you may have to be more creative. Many of these type of mouldings are available in poplar only, because the wood has the right characteristics to manufacture the pattern. Poplar does not blend well with other woods unless the piece is to take a dark stain. Try a few sample pieces first to see if it will blend with your

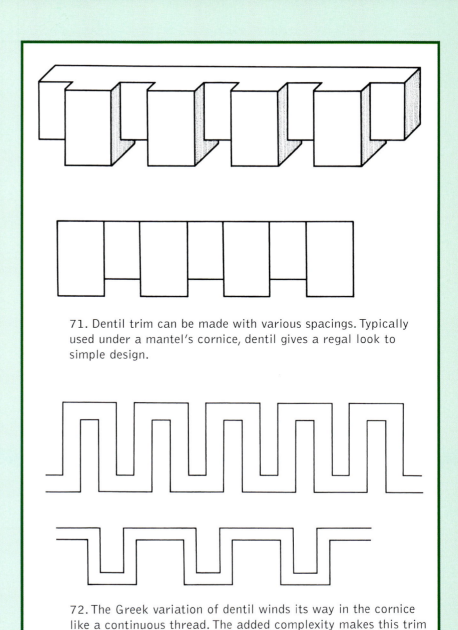

71. Dentil trim can be made with various spacings. Typically used under a mantel's cornice, dentil gives a regal look to simple design.

72. The Greek variation of dentil winds its way in the cornice like a continuous thread. The added complexity makes this trim hard to paint, yet provides a totally different look.

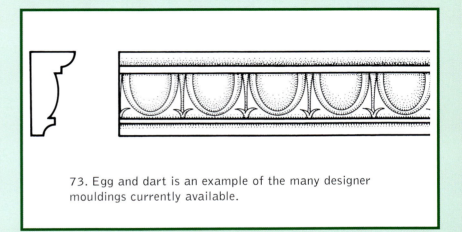

73. Egg and dart is an example of the many designer mouldings currently available.

74. Appliqués are highly decorative applied mouldings that create a hand-carved appearance. Readily available, they are easily applied with glue and brads.

75. Round columns provide a distinctive look for pilasters. They allow the designer to implement many features of classic design. Both large and small diameters will dictate the path of design for the entire surround.

other components. Always experiment before committing to a certain design.

ACCESSORIES

Keystones are a traditional element found in many fireplace settings (Figure 76). They can either be used as an applied moulding or integrated into the framework of the mantel. Columns, capitals, and corbels are other ways to dress up a mantel. These provide a distinctive Grecian look. Columns (Figure 75) can be a dominant feature by acting as the pilaster itself (either full round or half round) or, by using a smaller diameter column, it becomes an accent to the overall design. If you have a lathe you can turn these yourself or simply purchase them. If the column is to have a decorative profile it will have to be constructed of solid wood. Many companies produce stock turnings for the furniture industry that can be used in this application.

If the column has a flat profile but is to be tapered, it too will require the use of solid wood, which may be purchased from a supplier. If the column has equal diameter throughout its length, you can use solid wood, plywood, or staved construction. Columns can also be square, although square columns are rarely used in mantels, except in modified pilaster form. In any case, when purchasing from a supplier, plan on modifying the column to fit your design. Pre-made columns are available in different forms (Figure 77). Staved construction, or finger-jointed, is composed of

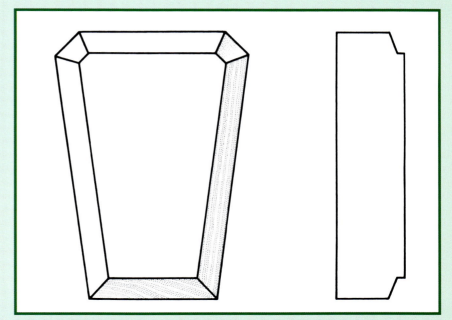

76. The keystone is a traditional fireplace element located in the center of the frieze above the firebox. Typically found in stone surrounds, the look is equally popular in wood applications.

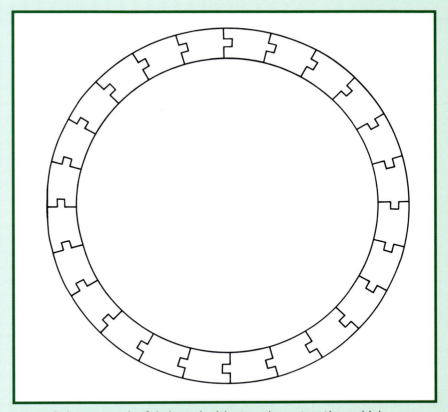

77. Columns can be fabricated with staved construction, which requires a miter cut on each piece to form the correct diameter. For added strength and ease of assembly, tongue-and-groove or spline joints can be used.

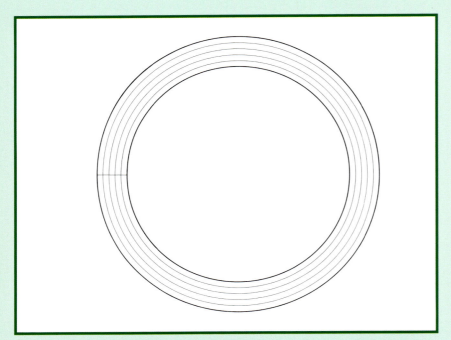

78. Curved plywood column construction is achieved by gluing veneers around a circular form. These are readily available in various diameters. Species selection is limited, but the initiated builder can easily veneer the column in the wood of choice.

79. Capitals cap the top of a column. Traditionally thought of as complex carvings, a hybrid example could be a square block or conventional use of crown moulding.

several pieces of wood that have been mitered, glued together, and turned into a cylinder. When purchased, staved construction will offer a limited amount of radiuses to choose from.

Curved plywood (Figure 78) is manufactured by bending thin plies around a form. Available in many radius options, its biggest drawback is that you can't add flutes, because flutes will expose the plies. Even with a painted mantel I would not recommend it. Solid wood is the best all-around choice, but also the most expensive and time-consuming to fabricate. If using a natural finish, it is hard to match the characteristics of solid wood. However, by veneering plywood and staved-type (pre-manufactured) columns with exotic veneers you can achieve stunning results with the minimal amount of labor. In order to do this effectively, you will need a good veneer press.

Capitals are simply caps that sit on top of a column. In mantel design, capitals act as the support for the cornice (Figure 79). If you don't like the column look but like the way the capital interacts with the shelf, use a corbel instead (Figure 80). Corbels are decorative braces that offer support to a member. These can be simple band-sawn pieces that are cut and routed, or ornate carved pieces that invite a closer look at the detail. If you want an ornate piece, once again, the easiest option is to consult a moulding supplier.

Don't let this list of mouldings overwhelm you. Mouldings are meant to be playful and manipulated. If you can't find the moulding you want, don't be afraid to cut and modify an available one. Let your eye discover what it likes, and modify or add mouldings together to achieve the desired appearance. Mouldings are like a pack of wolves. In design, they are manageable as single units, yet often overwhelming with many. In application, they have simple beauty as individuals; grouped together, they exude dominance and command attention. ◦

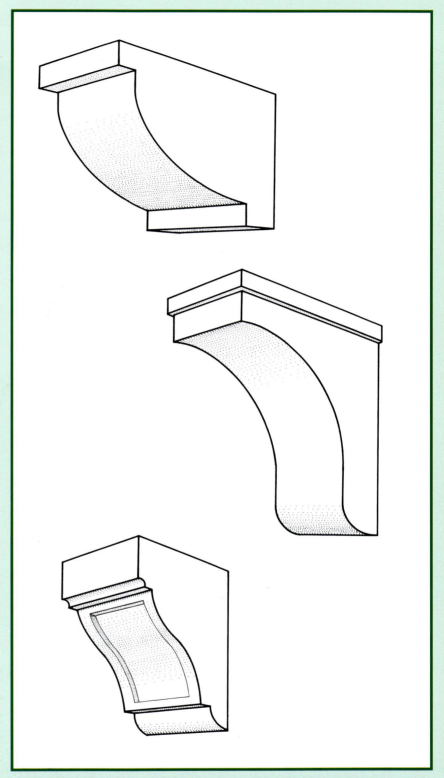

80. Corbels are brackets that support a shelf. Simple corbels can easily be hand fabricated. Complex designs can be purchased from suppliers.

81. Ceramic tile has been a popular choice in mantel slips ever since the material was made available. Tile can be a bold, dominant force as in this example, or used as an accent to other elements.

CHAPTER 5

Non-Combustible Materials Used Around Fire Boxes

A NON-COMBUSTIBLE WALL is one that will not catch fire easily or conduct heat. Choices for non-combustible materials are as equally unlimited as your wood selection. To name a few: brick, natural stone, ceramic tile, concrete, plaster, and glass. In addition to the different types of materials, within each group you'll also find a choice of textures. For instance, brick can have either a smooth or rough face. Stone could be in a natural cut slate, smooth polished granite, or the softer-looking dull limestone or marble. The finish on ceramic tiles varies from high-gloss glazes to textured matte finishes and everything in between. Although concrete typically has a smooth finish on interior surfaces, it can easily be given a coarse look by manipulating it in its fluid state, or by embedding other materials in it. To further complicate the choice of material, you can mix different types of non-combustibles to achieve a unique look. As you can see, the wide range of non-combustible choices requires you to first decide what type of look you're trying to achieve (Chapter 2) before you purchase material for the job.

82. Brick veneer is one of the most common materials used for the non-combustible surface. In this well-designed example, it was also incorporated into the mantel surround itself.

Wood is inherently warm-looking, smooth, and inviting to touch. We also understand that products made from wood need regular attention to be kept looking good for years. Non-combustible materials are essentially the opposite. They don't need to be cared for in the same way wood does. You can place concrete and stone outside with minimal maintenance and no fear of rotting. Both have a reputation of being strong, permanent, and un-moveable. These are the characteristics of a good building foundation. Because of that, we tend to associate all non-combustibles as strong and permanent materials. However, unlike the rarely seen foundation of a house, the hard material you select around your fireplace has the potential to become the focal point of the room. Most non-combustibles share the trait of being cold and hard, but since it is a finish material, it needs to be inviting to the touch. Choose this material wisely. Although the mantel surround is not always centered around the stonework slip, it is a marriage that requires cooperation with the wood surround. Use it as an accent to your piece. Don't let it take over unless your mantel design specifically calls for it. An example of this would be a simple shelf in a large river rock fireplace.

If the surround is meant to display your woodworking prowess, the stone work must be subtle and relegated to a supporting role.

Brick veneer is probably the most common material found as the design element in fireplaces (Figure 82). When a builder leaves the fireplace naked and unclothed (without a mantel), brick is often the material of choice. It is traditional, satisfies the non-combustible requirements, and doesn't require another trade (finish carpenter) to be involved with the fireplace construction. An advantage to installing a mantel over brick is its relatively flat surface. The straight edges of the wooden mantel surround fit nicely over the mason's handiwork. Other than that, brick is rarely designed into a retrofit mantel. More often than not, mantels end up covering the brick that was meant to be the center of attention. This is the result of an original fireplace brickwork that had no intention of having a mantel. If you have an existing brick wall that you choose to highlight because of its unique texture, color or masonry detail (i.e., arched firebox, recycled brick highlighting rustic decor, etc.), you will want to keep the brick exposed between the firebox and mantel surround, and possibly even beyond the pilaster and cornice. If the brick is boring and a nuisance to the design, you may wish to cover the brick with another non-combustible material around the firebox. Exposed brick far enough away from the firebox so that it is not a fire hazard, can be covered with any material, such as wood paneling or a framed sheetrock wall. Brick is better known as a building material than finished stone. Hence, it will usually be worked around, rather than into the design.

Rough stone fireplaces like river rock are very popular in rustic settings (Figure 83). These pose interesting challenges for mantels. The rock is varied and not on the same plane. This is why mantels in these locations are often simple timbers creating a shelf; mantels become an accent to the rock, rather than trying to conceal it. This is because the rock is the design emphasis. If the rough stone look is what you want, you

83. River rock fireplaces can be challenging for the mantel builder. Usually designed for rustic settings, the mantel is often best left simplified.

aren't limited to cutting and fitting individual pieces of the actual material. Manufactured stone panels are available in many different forms that have dramatically reduced the labor intensity. River rock, flagstone, and various brick patterns come in either prefabricated panels or individual stones with the backs pre-cut flat for easy installation. Installation usually requires a cement board backer

(Wonderboard or Hardibacker) nailed to the studs or screwed to an existing masonry wall. Next, a thin-set mortar bed or other recommended adhesive is applied and the stones are set in place. Cutting is done with a hammer and cold chisel (stone) or masonry saw (brick patterns). The final step is to apply the mortar (or grout) between the stones or panels. If you are a purist and can't bear to

84. For those who like natural materials, stone offers the most options. Stone can be installed either as cut tiles or in the more natural slab form. Natural stone slips lend an air of elegance to the entire fireplace setting.

use artificial stone, the real thing is for you. Unless you're handy with masonry techniques, you'll need to hire a craftsman for this portion.

Ceramic tile is a very popular choice around fireplace boxes (Figure 81, page 62). It is cost-effective and relatively easy to install. As with all stone products, use a cement board substrate or an existing brick veneer face to apply the tiles to. Tiles are cut with a tile saw or cutter and arranged in the pattern of choice. If you plan your mantel and slip carefully, you may be able to arrange the tiles with minimal cutting.

Since there are so many choices, tile work can create spec-tacular designs. Patterns, solids, and even custom artwork can be found in enamel finish. Accent strips and pieces that are equally varied in color and patterns such as rope, bead and tuck, and rosettes present many more pos-sibilities. In addition, ceramic tiles are available in square and rectan-gular shapes. Find a good designer showroom and spend time reviewing your options. Don't for-get you will have grout lines with tile. Although size of the grout line (which depends on tile) and the color of grout can be altered, the lines will be visible. Consider grout lines when making the deci-sion to use ceramic tile. Whether they are subtle or dominant, they become a part of the overall design appearance.

Natural stone is my favorite (Figure 84). Because it is a natural product, color and pattern varies with each piece, and stone greatly compliments any wood mantel. In addition to the inherent beauty it lends to the mantel's appearance, it provides all the qualities of a non-combustible product. There are a number of choices. Granite, which typically has a decorative stony look, is generally polished to a high sheen that brings out its best characteristics. Marble is a very elegant stone with soft lines and grain. Marble looks good both

85. Non-combustible materials do not have to be limited to their traditional location. Used as a cornice shelf, this absolute black granite slab ties the material to the slip below.

polished and in a matte finish. Limestone, which is similar in appearance to marble, usually has a matte, unpolished look. All of these stones will typically be flat cut, creating a smooth surface. Slate, on the other hand, is a very rough material. The face is typically textured and uneven, causing the thickness of each piece to vary. In addition, the color and pattern within the same type of slate can vary greatly. Slate is a great choice if you want a stone appearance that is left in a natural, un-fashioned state.

Natural stone is available in two forms: tiles and slab. Tiles are natural stone pieces that have been pre-cut into squares, commonly 12-inch x 12-inch. At a half-inch thick, these tiles are slightly thicker than the 1/4-inch thick ceramic tiles. This will need to be accounted for when designing your mantel. Hard to cut, you'll need a diamond-cutting saw to size them. Grout lines are smaller than on ceramic, which gives a cleaner look. Slab, on the other hand, is one piece of 3/4-inch or thicker stone. It can be used both as the perimeter stone (or slip) around the firebox and as a mantel shelf (Figure 85). Slab is not a do-it-yourself project since it requires special tooling and experience to achieve good results.

First, it is very heavy and usually requires a couple of people to handle the material. To cut the slab to size, one needs a large specialty saw typically found only in commercial shops. The fabrication process does not stop there. Even if you had someone else cut the pieces to size for you, you still have to treat the edges. Visible edges are often profiled. Exposed cuts need to be polished. If the edge is to be thicker than the 3/4-inch slab, it will have to be built up by epoxying two pieces together. Even with the necessary experience, slab work is a daunting task.

The options for using stone do not have to be limited to the typ-

86. Slips don't have to be boring. Laser cut, interlocking granite pieces transform this slip from the ordinary to the unique. Notice how the hearth has been cut back at a 45-degree angle.

ical square shapes. A very elegant look can be achieved by cutting stone into decorative pieces that interlock with each other (Figure 86). Although still expensive, current precision laser-cutting technology has made this more affordable.

Concrete is another choice that is gaining popularity (Figure 87). The look is bold, brash and intentionally massive. The most typical applications I have seen have been for hearths and mantel shelves. A creative person could also incorporate concrete around the firebox as a complete surround. In its plastic state, concrete can be molded into a wide variety of forms and shapes. Stamping, or imprinting the concrete with a decorative tool, is another option. Stamps are available commercially, or you can fashion your own. If you were good at making mud pies as a child, you'll soon discover that talent transfers itself to concrete stamping. Concrete can also be colored to counteract its image as the gray behemoth. To use concrete around a mantel you must first shed the concept that it can be used as a foundation material only. Since concrete is formed for each project, its texture and appearance can easily be manipulated. Although it is not good for every application, it's a great choice for the right location.

In addition to the above, metal, cultured marble, solid-surface products such as Corian, and pre-cast plaster and stone can be integrated into a mantel. Metals are most commonly seen on fireplace inserts with an attached shroud.

87. Although gaining in popularity, most craftsmen don't consider concrete to be a finish material. This example shows an entire surround formed of concrete. Concrete can also be colored, or used more sparingly, such as for the slip or hearth only.

Don't however, think the use of metal is limited strictly to an insert or free-standing wood stove. Some fireplaces integrate metal in the form of a hood over the firebox. Custom metal panels can be fabricated around the jamb in lieu of stone to give the mantel a distinct look. If you do choose to use a metal panel slip, the material under the metal must also be non-combustible; heat will rapidly transfer from the metal to the material behind. The UBC is very specific about any combustible material near the firebox. Another option would be to use art metals such as pre-stamped pieces or custom fabrications as accents in a wood surround.

Cultured marble and solid-sur-face materials like Corian are manufactured products that simulate the appearance of stone. Since their characteristics are different, they should never be thought of as a substitute for stone, but rather an alternative in the right application. Because cultured marble and granite must be pre-cast by a commercial shop, its use will be limited by each shop's capabilities. In addition, cultured marble is not non-combustible, so it cannot be used for slips and hearths. Solid-surface materials offer greater options because the pieces are glued and fabricated into the desired design, rather than being cast in a form. Pieces are easily shaped with common woodworking tools making design possibilities endless. Corian boasts of having a Class I flammability rating but is still not considered non-combustible. Therefore, its use must be kept to either the surround elements or mantel shelf only. Some gas inserts and zero-clearance fireplaces may allow the use of these combustible stone imitations as slips. Be sure to check the manufacturer's recommendations and your local building department for proper certification. In addition, most solid-surface manufacturers require a certified fabricator just to purchase their materials. This further limits the do-it-yourselfer from using these products.

Other options would be using pre-cast materials. Many parts and even whole mantels can be

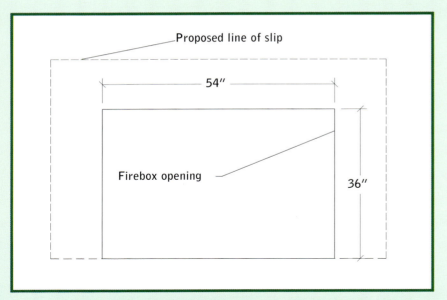

Proposed line of slip

54"

Firebox opening

36"

88. This drawing shows the firebox dimensions needed to lay out a tile mantel slip. Along with these dimensions, you'll need to know the size of the tiles that are being used.

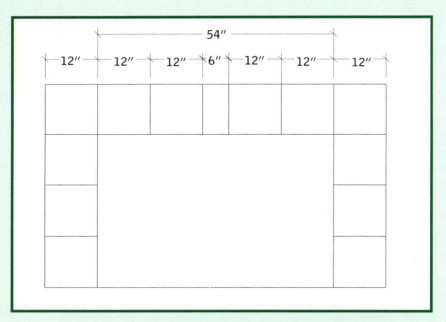

54"

12" 12" 12" 6" 12" 12" 12"

89. Cut tile centered in the slip is a pleasing solution. This example uses standard tile dimensions to its advantage by having to cut only one tile in the center of the frieze slip.

ordered made from pre-cast plaster and stone. If, for instance, you are looking for ornate, paint-grade corbels, this may be the way to go. Considerably cheaper than hand-carved woods, these products give you a lot of detail for a nominal cost. Check with the manufacturer on fire ratings. Some of these products may not be non-combustible.

TILE INSTALLATION

Before tile can be set, you must first do the layout. If the slip is to be 12 inches wide, measure the width of the firebox and add 12 inches to each side for the overall dimension (Figure 88). Draw level and plumb lines to form the outline of the tile slip. Opinions vary on tile substrate preparation. Some tilesetters install directly on the drywall. Others insist on removing the drywall and replacing with 1/2-inch cement board. The latter is more work, yet is better for installation.

Tile can be laid in many different configurations. For a traditional layout, the vertical jamb members of the slip will line up with the horizontal or header slip pieces. In this layout, you would divide the firebox opening width by 12 (the width of the tiles) to find the number of full tiles that will fit in the horizontal run. If the horizontal width of the firebox is 54 inches, you could have four (even number) full 12-inch tiles and one center tile cut to 6 inches (Figure 89). This type of layout will only work when you have an equal number of full tiles, so the cut tile is in the center of the opening. If however you have a horizontal opening of 66 inches, there would be five (odd number) full tiles at 12 inches and one tile to be cut at 6 inches. This would put the cut tile off-center and throw off the balance of the layout (Figure 90). To remedy this, keep the two end-tile widths at 12 inches to match the jamb, and divide the opening dimension into six equal tiles measuring 11 inches (Figure 91). The key is to create balance.

Secure a straight, level board at the top of the firebox opening to provide a support shelf for the tiles you're about to set. Next, using a notched trowel, apply a heat-resistant adhesive or quality thin-set mortar (check with your supplier) on the tile back and press into place on your layout lines. Place shim spacers between the tiles and proceed around the opening. When the thin-set has dried overnight, you are ready to finish the job with grout. Mix the grout according to the label. Using a sponge trowel, force the grout into all of the cracks between the tiles; scrape off the excess. After the material has had time to set up (follow package instructions), sponge the residue off the surface of the tiles. ◦

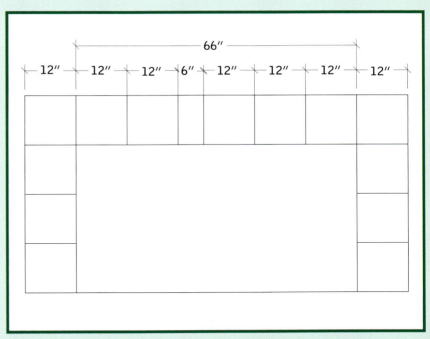

90. If the dimensions of the opening don't work well with the tile dimensions, more cutting will be required. A cut tile off-center is not an option for the slip layout.

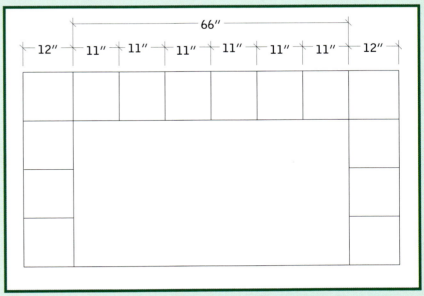

91. Cutting all tiles to an equal dimension is a much better solution. The goal is to create balance.

92. Rookwood tile fireplace with Honduran mahogany paneled room. Fireside room, Sorrento Hotel, Seattle, WA, circa 1908.

CHAPTER 6

Gallery of Mantels

IN THE FOLLOWING PAGES YOU WILL SEE a wide variety of mantels: simple to complex, stone to wood. Some designs are within the grasp of the do-it-yourselfer and others require the capabilities of a skilled craftsman. One thing they all have in common are ideas. Whether it is the use of mouldings, pilasters, stone, color, or the mixed use of materials, ideas can be gleaned for your own project.

Study the following photographs. Look for elements in each photo that speak to you positively or negatively. Critique the design and use of material. Use this as an exercise in recognizing objects that work, and those that don't. As you train yourself in the pages of this book you'll be better prepared to make these observations in the real world. Once you learn to notice the different elements of mantel design (and why they were implemented), you'll be on the road to creating a mantel that works for you.

93, 94. Circassian walnut carpentry done by Austrian craftsmen, carvings by Belgian wood carvers, circa 1903.

95. Vertical grain fir mantel with frame and flat panel construction. Raised limestone hearth.

96. Stone surround and chimney breast with hooded detail. Outside patio, circa 1903.

97. Rookwood tile fireplace with swan pattern, circa 1903.

98. Rookwood tile fireplace depicts a castle scene. Ceramic corbels and shelf, circa 1903.

99. Italian tile fireplace. Painted
white surround with decorative
corbels, pink and lavender
mouldings, circa 1903.

100. Arched ceramic tile fireplace with raised hearth and simple wood cornice shelf.

101. Walnut surround with granorex tile slip.

102. Mottled makore veneers with Honduras mahogany trims. Absolute black granite shelf, hearth and laser-cut granite slip.

103. Painted mantel surround with beaded mouldings, circa 1904.

104. Hand-made dragon andirons and carved lions support a crenelated hood, circa 1901.

105. Italian blue glass tile with carved leaf and vine mantel. Sycamore paneling. Painted medieval scenes on corduroy frieze above, circa 1901.

106. River rock fireplace with cedar log mantel shelf.

107. Painted wood mantel shelf with corbels, originally natural Douglas fir, circa 1904.

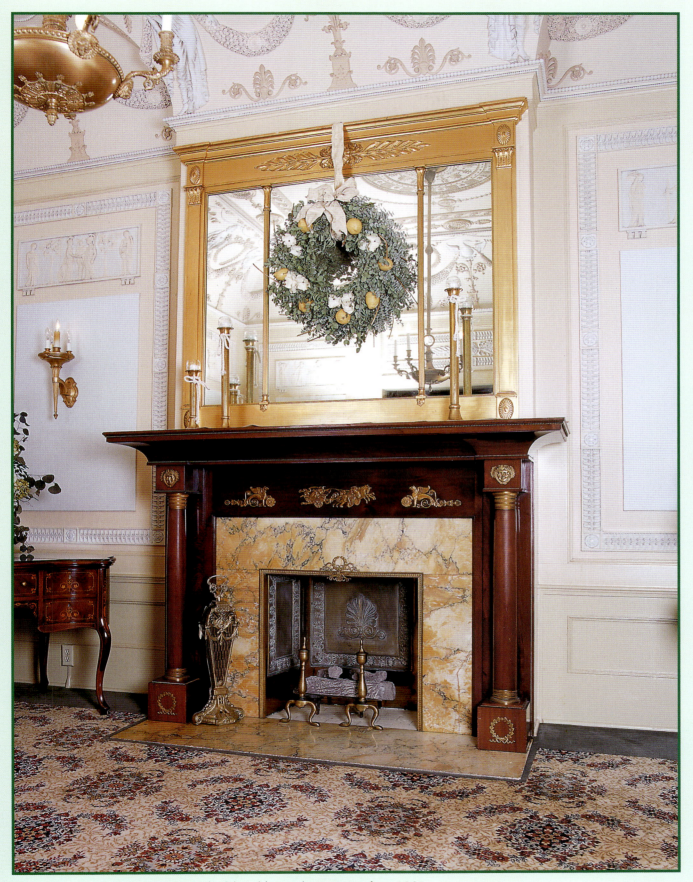

108. Ornamental mahogany mantel with gold ormolu mounts, circa 1901.

109. Painted mantel on a traditional fireplace wall with cabinet storage.

110, 111. Painted mantel over manufactured fireplace with no chimneybreast. Detail photo shows dentil trim, rosette, through beaded pilaster and plinth block.

112, 113. Ceramic tile surround with raised firebox and painted wood mouldings.

114. Nine-piece concrete mantel surround. Cap is one piece.

115. Eastern hardrock maple mantel piece with round column pilasters. Granite tile slip and hearth.

116. Painted mantel surround with painted wainscot. Granite tile slip and hearth.

117. Painted mantel with through fluted pilasters, plinth block and decorative wood appliqués. Marble tile slip and hearth.

118. Decorative brick fireplace wall.

119. Vertical grain fir mantel with parting bead.

120. Brick fireplace surround and shelf with wood cabinetry matching arched detail.

121. Rookwood tile fireplace with walnut bookshelves, circa 1903.

122. Detailed woodwork, circa 1903.

123. This simple painted mantel converted a brick face into a slip. It also acts as the bridge between a hickory entertainment center on the right, and display shelving on the left. The cabinetry projects 2 feet out from the wall, but is within the Uniform Building Code guidelines.

124. Oak mantel shelf over brick chimneybreast with oak cabinetry.

125. Painted mantel with arched raised panels on brick chimneybreast with raised hearth.

126. Whitewashed flat maple corner mantel installed around a pre-fabricate fireplace. Marble slip and hearth.

127. Honduras mahogany flat panel mantel and cabinetry with marble slip and hearth. Not wanting to crowd the fireplace, the entertainment center was set in the corner at 45 degrees

128. Book-matched mahogany paneling dominates this grand dining room. Carrying the theme to the mantel makes the fireplace part of the room, rather than an isolated element. Its recessed alcove is reminiscent of popular Arts & Crafts inglenook designs. ●

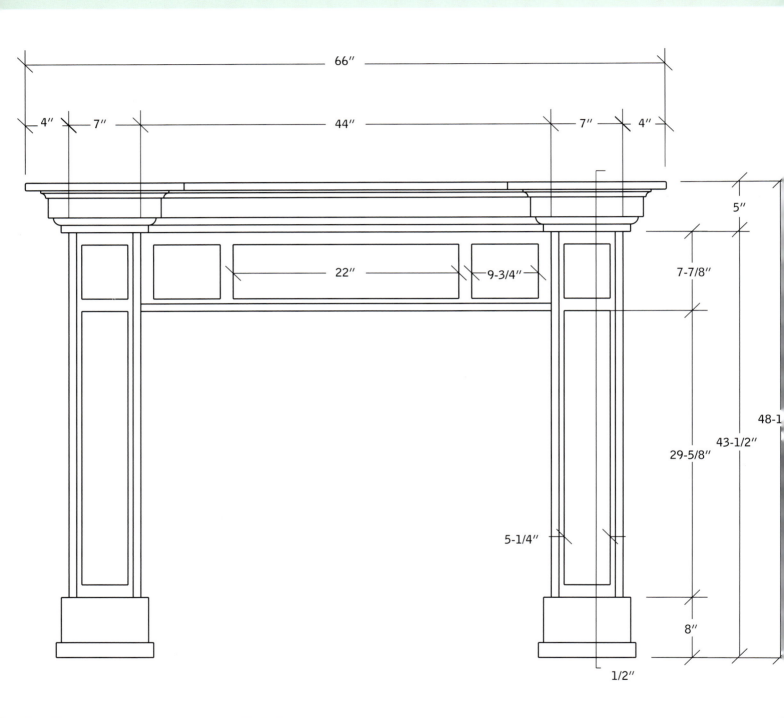

129. Elevation shop drawing of the off-the-shelf mantel project. Notice that all dimensions are listed for easy reference in the shop. Scaled drawings like this help the designer determine how well the design has been executed.

Fabricating an "Off-the-Shelf" Mantel

THE FIRST PROJECT WE WILL WALK through is what I'm calling an "off-the-shelf" mantel. Although there are many off-the-shelf wood-profiled mouldings available, I've elected to design this project using predominately square stock. This will create a Craftsman-style piece. The idea behind this project is to encourage those of you who don't have a lot of tools, experience, or time, yet want to build your own mantel. Good mantel design does not depend upon fancy mouldings and labor- intensive details. Sometimes, simplicity works the best. We'll discuss how to build this uncomplicated, solid wood mantel with materials readily available in most home centers and lumber yards. The joinery will be simple, and accomplished with a minimum of tools.

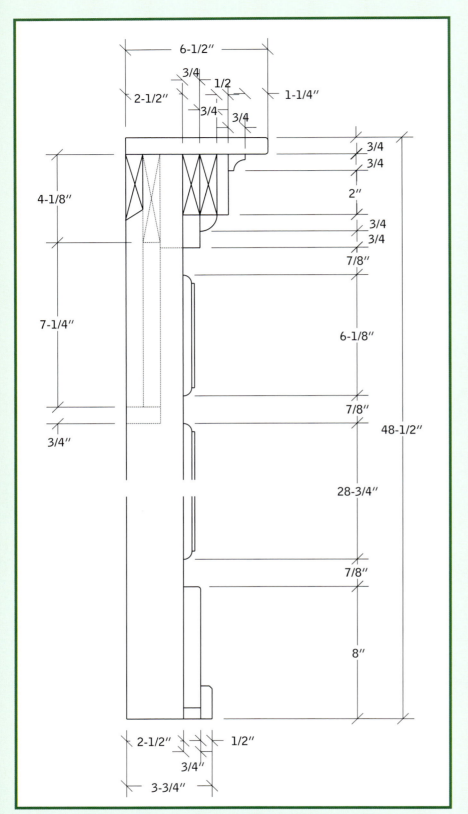

6-1/2"
3/4
1/2
2-1/2"
1-1/4"
3/4
3/4

4-1/8"

3/4
3/4

2"

3/4
3/4
7/8"

7-1/4"

6-1/8"

7/8"

3/4"

48-1/2"

28-3/4"

7/8"

8"

2-1/2"
1/2"
3/4"
3-3/4"

130. Section shop drawing of the off-the-shelf mantel project. This is a critical drawing for the builder. Extensive use of built-up mouldings requires explanation. Sections do just that—they explain the relationship between the various mantel parts.

Before designing a mantel, it is critically important to understand what materials are available and where to acquire them. Familiarizing yourself with different types of materials must precede design. Try window shopping at several lumber yards. Talk to sales people. Make it your mission to find out as much as you can about the material. Panel products machine differently than solid wood, as do different wood species. Getting acquainted with materials is like making new friends. It takes time and effort, yet yields a harvest of support. This support will aid you greatly in the planning process.

The shopping experience is one of my favorite parts of a project. This is where you select the raw materials that create the vision. Nothing yet has been cut, labored over, or damaged. Only the anticipation of starting a new project dominates your mind. Just simple raw materials. At this stage in the game you should have some idea of what you want to accomplish. Going to the lumber yard to see what they stock and how much your project will cost will greatly aid the design process. For this project, I selected a solid, vertical-grain fir mantel because it will match the rest of the millwork in the house. Here in the Northwest, vertical-grain (VG) fir and hemlock dimensioned lumber are readily available. In addition, the most common natural wood moulding available is hemlock. For that reason, many new homes provide hemlock moulding as a natural wood choice. After talking to a couple of lumber suppliers, you will soon find out what is readily available in your area. For the pilasters, I'll use a combination 1 x 6 and two 1 x 3's (Figure 129, page 96) for the side return. The base block will be 1 x 6 with a 1 x 2 base shoe. The frieze will be composed of a 1 x 8 and 1 x 2 return, along with additional 1 x material and 1/2-inch quarter round that will create an applied panel with moulding. For the cornice we'll play with a 1 x 8 as the horizontal shelf, and a combination of 1 x material to create a built-up moulding (Figure 130).

When shopping for lumber, you need to know how to recognize quality. There is nothing more frustrating than to encounter problems in the shop related to poor lumber. When working with dimensioned lumber, it is critical that you select your material carefully because it has already been surfaced to its final dimensions. For instance, the 1 x 6 we are using for the pilasters actually measures 3/4-inch x 5-1/2-inch. Rough lumber, on the other hand, would be close to the full 1 x 6 dimension. Although rough lumber requires more work to prepare, it allows you to machine many of the defects out. The first step is to check moisture content (described in the sidebar). Next, visually inspect the surface, looking for knots (Figure 132), checks, cracks (Figure 133), and undesirable grain patterns. The board doesn't have to be perfectly clean, but you need to be able to cut the defects out. That's why it is helpful to know the basic dimensions of your mantel before purchasing the lumber.

Kiln-Dried Lumber

Although most finish lumber is sold "kiln-dried," this is no guarantee it is ready to be worked. Kiln-dried lumber goes through a manufacturing process where green lumber is placed in heated kilns to remove moisture. This procedure stabilizes the wood so it can be fashioned without fear of movement created by moisture. If lumber is stored improperly, such as outside or in an unheated warehouse, it will draw in moisture like a sponge. Whenever you work with solid wood, check the moisture content of the wood. A good rule of thumb is between 6% and 8%. The higher the moisture content, the more seasonal change will affect the wood. This will also be determined in part by your climate. For instance, if during fabrication you used wood with a high moisture content and installed the mantel in a dry home (especially by a fireplace), then once the wood equalizes to its environment (loses moisture) it will begin to move. The wood can split, pop joints open, and generally wreak havoc on a finished piece of millwork. A moisture meter is a good investment because it warns you of potential problems before you begin fabrication. Although there are many different types available, they all work basically the same. Insert the prongs into each board in several locations to determine its moisture content (Figure 131). If you don't have a moisture meter, purchase lumber that has been kept inside. Make every effort to store and fabricate it in an environment (temperature and humidity) that is similar to where it will ultimately reside.

131. Moisture content in wood must always be considered. An inexpensive meter like this one will reveal how much moisture the wood has in it. Be sure to check several places in each board.

132. Knots, unless part of a rustic design, are considered defects. Tight knots are those that have not compromised the integrity of the wood surface and can often be left in. Loose knots fall out, require extensive repair, and are best avoided.

133. Checks are failures in the wood grain caused by released tension. Cracks are checks that occur along the edge of a board. Both are problematic and need to be tossed.

134. When a board curves along the grain of the wood it is called a bow. Besides jointing a bow out of a board, it can be dealt with in two ways. First, cut into shorter pieces to remove the bow or second, if the board is secured along it's entire length, the bow can be tamed.

135. Don't rely on inspecting a board's face to determine quality. Defects such as bowing and twisting can only be detected when looking at a board along its edge.

136. Cupping occurs when a board curves against the grain direction. Using a straight edge is the best way to determine how badly it is cupped. A tape measure can be used as a quick straightedge.

137. When a board has a twist or diagonal bend in it, discard it. Imagine trying to straighten out an aluminum can that has been twisted. Better to buy a new one than waste your time with this defect.

Finally, inspect for bowing, cupping, and twisting. Bowing is when a board curves along the grain of the wood (Figure 134). This is very common with dimensioned lumber, so you need to check every board. Look down the length of the board (Figure 135) to determine how badly it is bowed. If a board has a minor bow it can often be used—if it will be secured to a straight edge of another board. If the bow is severe, it will be problematic and should be avoided. Cupping is when a board bends against the grain of the wood. You can visually detect this at the end of a board, but you'll need a straight edge to check in the middle of a board. I use the edge of a tape measure to check for cupping (Figure 136). Cupping greater than 1/16 inch in dimensioned lumber should be rejected.

Twisting is the worst of the defects. This is when a board is bent along the diagonal of the grain (Figure 137). Glance down along the length of the board and you'll notice the edges curl down if there is a twist. Unless you can joint and plane the twist out, reject it. Twisted boards are very aggravating to work with and are better left at the lumber yard.

A final note on shopping for lumber. Some yards discourage customers from selecting their own lumber, understandable when you consider liability issues and the fact that some people disrupt the neat piles of lumber. However, you must insist on examining the lumber yourself if you want to ensure quality. Lumber yards worth purchasing from are ones that will

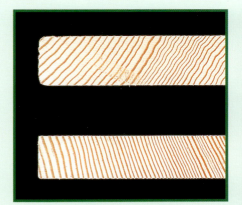

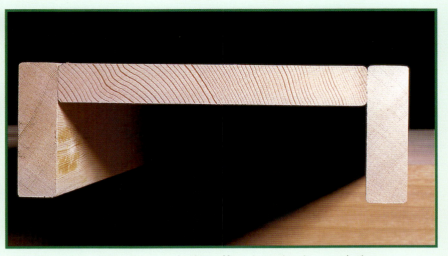

138. Much of the dimensioned lumber purchased today will have a slight ease along the edge, as shown in the top board of the photo. The bottom board has been surfaced square without the manufacturer's rounded edge.

139. To avoid cutting the eased edge off, we're using it as a design element. When two eased edges are joined they form a quirk. Joints that incorporate a quirk are forgiving because the mating pieces do not have to line up exactly.

140. Factory-eased edges are not always consistent. To ensure they are, or to ease your own, run a block with sandpaper down the edge to form the slight radius.

141. Using biscuits as the spline joint requires accurate placement of the slots. Mark the biscuit locations on one board.

142. Hold the mating piece up to the first board and transfer the pencil layout marks. For the pieces to line up properly, the biscuit cutter must be indexed off the side where both pieces mate.

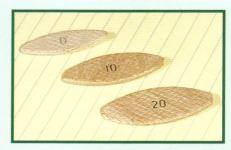

143. Biscuits come in three standard sizes: #0, being the smallest, #10, and #20. Use #10 in 1/2" material and #20 in 3/4" and thicker. #0 are handy for narrow locations that won't allow the larger slots.

144. Cutting the biscuit slots is fast and simple. Just make certain you hold the tool firmly, square and flat to the surface.

136. After adding a small bead of glue along the board's edge, line up the mating boards at one end. Place each biscuit in its slot and drive it home.

145. Getting the right amount of glue is tricky. I put it in the slot with a slight wiggle of the biscuit to ensure full coverage. Too much glue leaves a mess and can make assembly difficult.

147. When the boards are properly aligned, clamp the assembly. Put scrap wood between the clamps and the assembly to prevent damage. Paper under the clamp bars will prevent discoloration caused by the metal coming in contact with the glue.

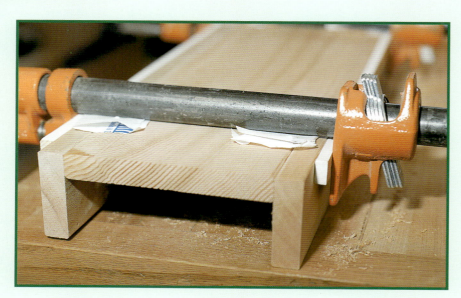

accommodate this request.

Starting with the pilasters, cut the 1 x 6 and 1 x 3 to the mantel height, minus the thickness of the top (3/4 inch). Next, attach the return pieces to the 1 x 6. Normally, I would conceal the joint at the sides, but in this application I want to accentuate it. I've chosen this detail because the edges of most dimensioned lumber are eased or rounded (Figure 138). If we wanted a flush joint, we would have to trim all edges square. Instead, we are going to use the eased edge to form a quirk, which is a mating joint detail (Figure 139). Run a sandpaper block along the edge of the board to be certain that the eased edge is consistent (Figure 140). Relying on glue and nails would be adequate, but a concealed spline is just as simple and better. Use biscuits for the spline. Mark the locations of the biscuits on both pieces with a 10 inch maximum spacing (Figure 141). Be sure you index the biscuit cutter from the mating side of both pieces to be joined (Figure 142). Biscuits are available in three sizes of #0, #10 and #20 (Figure 143). Cut all slots for the large #20 biscuit (Figure 144). Next, put glue in the slots prior to the biscuits and run a small bead the length of the joint, keeping it on the back side of the biscuit slots (Figure 145). Square up the bottom and top (Figure 146), and clamp together. Use a block of wood between the clamp and finished piece (Figure 147) to prevent damage to the material and to apply an even pressure throughout the joint. In addition, placing small pieces of paper

148. Our design calls for the pilasters to project out 1 inch from the frieze.

149. Since the frieze blocking will not be seen, I have chosen a quick method of attachment. Pocket holes, while unsightly, are very effective. Cutting them with a pocket hole cutter is fast and easy.

150. Apply a bead of glue along the edge of the blocking. Place a clamp over the joint to hold the two pieces flush and tight to each other. A pan head pocket screw securely fastens the blocking to the top.

151. Blocking must be attached to the back of each frieze end. This is a stress joint, so use both glue and screws.

152. Pre-drill the blocking in the pilaster legs to eliminate the possibility of splitting the wood, and to help the two pieces stay aligned while attaching. This is because you are not pushing a screw out of the first board, but only screwing into the second board, which pulls the joint tightly together.

153. Apply glue with a brush. Be certain to get full spread coverage.

154. Line the pieces up and place one clamp over the joint using light pressure. Double check positioning of the pieces and tap into place as needed with a hammer. Tighten the clamp.

155. Attach a second clamp, paying careful attention to the alignment. Secure the assembly with wood screws.

156. Since the mantel assembly is going to be moved around the shop, attach a stretcher board to the bottom of the pilasters. By tacking a piece of scrap plywood on the surround, you can safely slide the unit around the shop and move it to the fireplace.

between the wood and clamp will help reduce staining caused by the pipe clamp.

Take the same approach for the frieze as for the pilasters but use a 1 x 2 as the return so it sits back 1 inch from the pilaster (Figure 148). Since the built-up moulding that serves as the crown has a net height of 4-1/4-inch (Figure 130, page 98), attach the blocking to the top of the frieze to accommodate the cornice crown. By adding a 3/4-inch x 4-1/8-inch piece of plywood to the top of the frieze, it is lowered to its correct location. Once applied, the cornice finish trims (4-1/4-inch overall height) conceal the plywood blocking joint. Using a pocket hole cutter (Figure 149), prepare the top blocking. Attach the top blocking with pocket screws (Figure 150), or biscuits and clamps. Next, add blocking to the backside of each frieze end (Figure 151); the lower mantel body parts are done. After the glue dries, sand the three components and flip them upside down for assembly. Next, pre-drill the holes (Figure 152), apply glue (Figure 153), line the ends up (Figure 154), and clamp and screw the unit together (Figure 155). The box will hold together but is not too stable on its own. So, before going any further, cut a stretcher board and attach it to the bottom of the pilaster legs for support (Figure 156). Omitting this step can surely end in tragedy. Not only will this stretcher help avert possible damage in handling, but will also allow you to slide the unit around the shop easier.

Now flip the mantel back over.

157. With the mantel surround flipped over, lay out the applied panels. Cut scrap lumber to the size of the proposed panels to help determine proper proportion.

158. At the top of the mantel, plywood blocking is installed. When placed on top of the blocking, the cornice trim will have greater depth. Attach with glue and staples or small nails.

159. Creating your own factory edge with a router gives consistent results. Use a 1/8-inch round overbit.

160. Accurate panel layout is critical. Measure equal distances and then mark with a square to ensure the panels stay parallel to the surround.

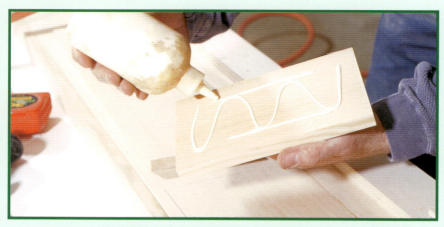

161. Apply glue to the panel back. By keeping the glue away from the panel edges, you eliminate glue squeeze-out that would have to be cleaned up later.

At this point you're ready to lay out the applied panels. Working from the dimensions on the drawing, mark out the panel locations. This step helps determine if the proportions look as good in the three-dimensional realm as they did on the two-dimensional drawing. For further help, cut some scrap wood to the dimensions of the panel to see if you like the layout (Figure 157). Next apply the 3/4-inch x 2-3/4-inch plywood top blocking (Figure 158) which makes the cornice trim project out further (Figure 130, page 98). Applying the blocking now helps in proportioning the applied panels. Once satisfied with the applied panel proportions, prepare the actual stock. Since a quirk runs the entire length of the pilaster, I don't want the applied panel to overlap this joint. The dimension between quirks is 5-1/2-inch (standard 1 x 6 dimension). By allowing 1/8-inch from each quirk, we'll need to subtract 1/4-inch from the entire width of the pilaster panels. This gives a net overall width of pilaster panel, including quarter round of 5-1/4-inch (Figure 129, page 96). With the 1/2-inch quarter-round as the edgebanding, subtract an additional inch off the width of the panel. The net width of the applied panel is therefore 4-1/4-inch.

Originally, I planned to use a standard 1 x 4 (3-1/2-inch wide) to simplify the panel preparation. I quickly changed that idea and opted for the wider panel after I discovered, through the scrap panel step, that the proportions were wrong. The grain of the frieze material runs horizontal and the pilaster grain runs vertical. This grain direction arrangement is fairly typical in solid lumber use. If all the grain were to run vertical, you would have to edge-glue several pieces together to achieve the proper frieze width–not a practical option unless you are using veneer. Therefore, the grain of all applied panels will run in the same direction as the members underneath them. Since the frieze is 7-1/4-inch wide (nominal 1 x 8), use a 1 x 6 (net 5-1/2-inch width) cut down to 5-1/8-inch for the applied frieze panels. Combining that width with the same 1/2-inch quarter-round, the panel measures 6-1/8-inch wide (Figure 130, page 98). Setting the panel back the identical 1/8-inch from the quirk line, leaves exactly 1 inch to the top of the fir frieze. The 1-1/2-inch fir cornice trim will overhang the blocking/fir transition joint by 1/8-inch, leaving the same 7/8-inch reveal that is found between all applied panels (Figure 130, page 98).

One more step before cross-cutting the panels: double-check your dimensions. Make sure you accounted for the 1/2-inch quarter-round when determining the length of the panel. Once all the panels are sized, sand the faces and edges. Since the cross cut will not have the factory-eased edge, you'll need to create this yourself either with an 1/8-inch radius round-over bit on the router (Figure 157) or sanded by hand. Lay out the panel location (Figure 160). To attach the panels, use a small amount of glue on the back (Figure 161), and pin-nail it with a pneumatic nailer, either from the

162. Using a small brad nailer, tack each panel down. Don't overdo the brads. They are only used to hold the panel in place until the glue dries.

163. If you don't have a brad gun, or surface nails are objectionable, panels can be attached from behind. Pre-drill the holes, clamp the panel in place and drive the screws home.

164. In some cases, you may not be able to screw, nail or clamp the panel while the glue dries. In that instance, use a couple dabs of hot-melt glue to hold the panel. Work fast; hot melt dries quickly and can form a lump under the panel.

165. Don't rely exclusively on your layout lines for panel attachment. To ensure all panels line up with each other, use a straight edge or square indexed off an adjoining panel, or use the box itself during installation.

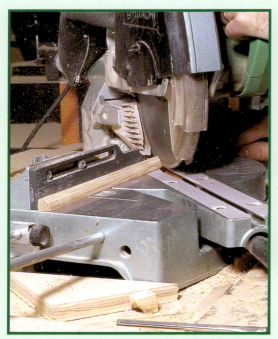

166. Since the saw motor blocks the view on left-hand cuts, I cut all left-hand miters of the panel edge first.

167. With the left-hand miter cut lined up against the panel end, mark the opposite panel end location on the edge banding. This will be the exact cut line for the right-hand miter.

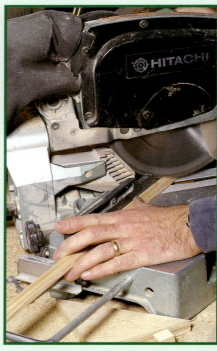

168. Cut the right-hand miter.

169. With a small amount of glue on the backside, pin-nail the edge banding around the panel.

front or back (Figure 162). Nailing can be done without a pneumatic nailer if you pre-drill the holes. You can also pre-drill and screw it from behind (Figure 163). Another alternative is to apply yellow glue with a couple dabs of hot-melt glue to hold the panel in place until the yellow glue is set (Figure 164). It's critical you attach these panels square to the box. This will ensure the panel edges line up parallel with the quirks (Figure 165). Now apply the quarter-round. Set up the miter saw and cut a series of left-side miters. I like to cut the left side first because the saw motor is on the right and obstructs the view of the left hand miter (Figure 166). Using this method of cutting allows you to make the cut more precisely, since you're relying on the panel itself as the ruler instead of a tape measure. Place the pieces next to the panels, lining them up with the corner and mark the right-hand miter cut (Figure 167). Make the right-hand cut on the saw (Figure 168) and work your way around the panel. Cutting all your pieces in this manner will assure good fitting joints. Apply a small dab of glue and pin nail on (Figure 169). Again, if you have to hand nail this step, pre-drill the holes to prevent splitting, or use hot melt glue on the back to hold the piece in place while the yellow glue dries.

Another alternative that will change the panel design is to use a 5/8-inch or 1/2-inch thickness instead of the standard 3/4-inch dimension. This reduces the projection of the panels, which is more appealing to some. If 5/8-inch or

170. Re-sawing lumber wider than 3 inches on a 10-inch table saw requires two cuts. Notice how the board has been flipped upside down with the first cut now on top.

171. Re-sawing lumber on the band saw is typically safer, faster and more accurate. Band saws have greater depth capacity and virtually no danger of kickback.

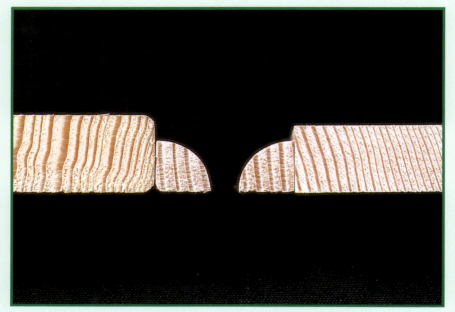

172. Panel thickness greatly influences design. The 3/4-inch panel on the left has the same 1/2-inch quarter round edge banding as the 5/8-inch panel does on the right. The distinction viewed from the panel face can be almost as dramatic.

173. Large miter cuts are done on the table saw. To reduce the amount of tear-out on the tail end of the cut, use a scrap piece of wood butted against the back of the finish board.

1/2-inch stock is not available, the ambitious can dimension the material either on a table saw, bandsaw, planer, or any combination. When using a table saw, do a double cut if your saw uses a 10-inch or smaller diameter blade (Figure 170); simply flip the board over to complete the cut. I prefer the bandsaw. It can make the cut in one pass, has less waste, and is generally safer (Figure 171). Set the fence a minimum 1/16-inch over the size of the final dimension so you can plane the board to its final thickness. If you don't have a planer, simply cut it to the net size. Even though this will leave one rough face, only the uncut face side will be visible. Plane to final thickness. For the example shown here, one panel is 3/4-inch thick and the second is 5/8-inch thick (Figure 172). Both have the same 1/2-inch x 1/2-inch perimeter edgebanding. Notice how changing this reveal dimension alters the look of the panel detail.

After you've given the glue ample time to dry–usually an hour or two–sand the quarter-round joints and fill any joints with putty, as required. Don't fill the nail holes as they can be better concealed with color putty after the project has been finished (Chapter 9).

Attach the base next. The 1 x 6 base should be mitered, as opposed to using a butt joint, so as not to reveal the end grain. Miter both ends of the front piece (Figure 173). Place a scrap block behind the blade to reduce tear-out when cutting. Align it with a mating miter return piece and attach it in the same manner as the applied panels. Cut two return pieces 12 inches long with a miter on both ends. Pre-fit and sand them to the attached face piece, but do not cut and attach them to the pilaster legs yet. By cutting and attaching them after the mantel is installed, you can achieve a tighter fit to the wall, as described in the scribing method below. At this point, just sand the 1 x 2. Do all the mitering during installation. Since it is a smaller dimension, the 1 x 2 is easily cut on site.

Much like Dr. Frankenstein must have felt, we now have the legs and trunk of our creation assembled. By attaching the head (or cornice), the anticipation of project completion is upon us. Rather than looking like an ugly monster, however, this will be adding a crown of dignity. This cornice shelf will invite warm conversation and special adornments. No scars here, unless we leave our mistakes to add character.

The cornice shelf we're using is a 1 x 8. This would imply a finish dimension of 7-1/4-inch. Since the pilasters project 2-1/2-inch from the wall (1 x 3), the shelf would then project 4 3/4-inch from the face of the pilasters (7-1/4-inch minus 2-1/2-inch). To make the cornice conform to the proportion of the mantel body, we need to add some bulk to the underside. This is commonly done through the use of crown moulding. On this mantel, however, we are going to simplify the design by using a series of basic stock lumber. My biggest concern with square stock lumber for the crown is making the cornice appear too top heavy.

174. Now the 3/4-inch plywood blocking is attached to the top. This piece sits behind the finish piece of lumber and is designed to create more depth for the cornice. All blocking is totally concealed by finish lumber.

175. With the compound saw set to a bevel of 45 degrees, miter cut the 1-1/2-inch wide bottom trim.

176. The bottom trim must conceal the joint between the top of the finish board and the plywood blocking. Set the trim 1/8 inch below the joint.

177. With glue and pin nails, work your way around the surround. Remember, nails should be used sparingly.

178. The 3/4-inch quarter round piece is the next to be installed. By this stage in the project, you will be a pro at mitering. Attaching this trim piece will seem like child's play.

179. The top 1/2- x 3-1/2-inch cornice trim will be the most noticeable. Take extra care in mitering for tight joints.

180. Small cracks and joints can be filled with wood putty. Using the right amount of putty takes practice. Too much and you will have to sand more later. Too little and it will require a second coat.

To reduce this affect we will trim the 1 x 8 shelf down to a net size of 6-1/2-inch.

Referring to Figure 130, page 98, we see our crown is made up of four individual pieces: 3/4-inch x 1-1/2-inch, 1/2-inch x 3-1/2-inch, 3/4-inch quarter- round and 3/4-inch cove moulding. Now attach the second piece of 3/4-inch plywood blocking that sits behind the 1/2-inch x 3-1/2-inch fir cornice moulding (Figure 174). Starting with the bottom 3/4-inch x 1-1/2-inch piece, miter all outside corners (Figure 175). Remember to set the bottom edge 1/8-inch below the plywood to conceal the joint (Figure 176). Glue and pin-nail the piece in place, working your way around the pilasters and frieze (Figure 177). As discussed with the base moulding, leave the wall-mitered return piece off until installation. This is recommended unless you are absolutely certain of a straight and uniform wall surface. Proceed in the same manner with the bottom 3/4-inch quarter-round (Figure 178). Attach the top 3-1/2-inch piece (Figure 179) and putty all necessary joints (Figure 180). Precut and fit the top cove moulding, but do not attach it. Both the top moulding and shelf are left loose to attach during installation. Lastly, cut the shelf down to its final net length. Measure the distance of the mantel width, add the dimension of the crown moulding pieces that were left off the ends (1/2-inch + 3/4-inch = 1-1/4-inch), add the dimension that the shelf overhangs the cove piece (1-1/4 inch), which gives you a 2-1/2 inch overhang each side. Multiply by two to achieve the net overall length of the shelf (Figures 129, page 96, and 130, page 98). After the shelf is cut, ease the shelf ends to match the front factory edge, as was done for the applied panel ends.

NOTE: It is also common practice to attach the shelf and all mouldings prior to installation. This method allows the builder to complete the fabrication in the shop, leaving the simple task of attaching the mantel surround to the wall. Shop joints and finishing are typically preferred over field work. Any mantel that is purchased pre-assembled or in a kit will usually be fabricated this way. If I am certain that the walls are flat and the mantel surround will fit tightly, or if pieces can be easily pre-scribed from templates, I will fabricate it as a complete unit. Working in older homes and even some newer ones with bowed and out-of-plumb walls can be daunting. It's generally easier to scribe the pieces on site. Certain mantel pieces are best field-applied, guaranteeing a tight, custom fit. Of all the millwork I've seen throughout the years, the stuff that looks the best is that which fits the tightest. With careful planning, fabrication, and installation techniques, one can achieve equal and sometimes superior results with field-applied parts. It is up to the discretion of each builder to decide how best to complete his project. ๏

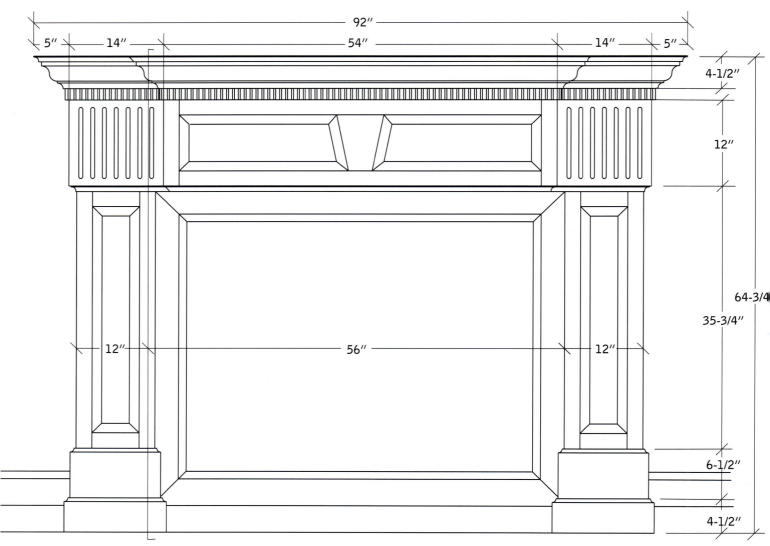

92″

5″ 14″ 54″ 14″ 5″

4-1/2″

12″

64-3/4″

35-3/4″

12″ 56″ 12″

6-1/2″

4-1/2″

Section line—see page 118

181. Shop drawing elevation of the custom painted mantel project. The more complex a project becomes, the more important the drawing is. Answering the many questions of design is difficult at best, but a good drawing goes a long way in providing answers.

CHAPTER 8

Fabricating a Complex Mantel

MANY OF THE TECHNIQUES AND applications used to fabricate the mantel in the previous chapter will be repeated here. This chapter, however, will cover the construction of a painted mantel with more complex joinery and parts. Remember, all mantel construction is centered around the basic elements of pilaster, frieze, and cornice. The embellishments that adorn the mantel create its uniqueness.

Because this is a painted mantel, we will use a combination of MDF (see discussion on medium density fiberboard in Chapter 5) and hardwood mouldings. Special care needs to be taken when constructing paint-grade pieces. The temptation is to get sloppy with joinery, thinking the application of spackle and caulk is an adequate remedy. An opaque paint actually magnifies all joinery, wood preparation (or lack thereof), and defects. The biggest advantage of a painted mantel is not having to worry about matching grain and species. It is worth noting, however, that you must pick appropriate species for painting (Chapter 5).

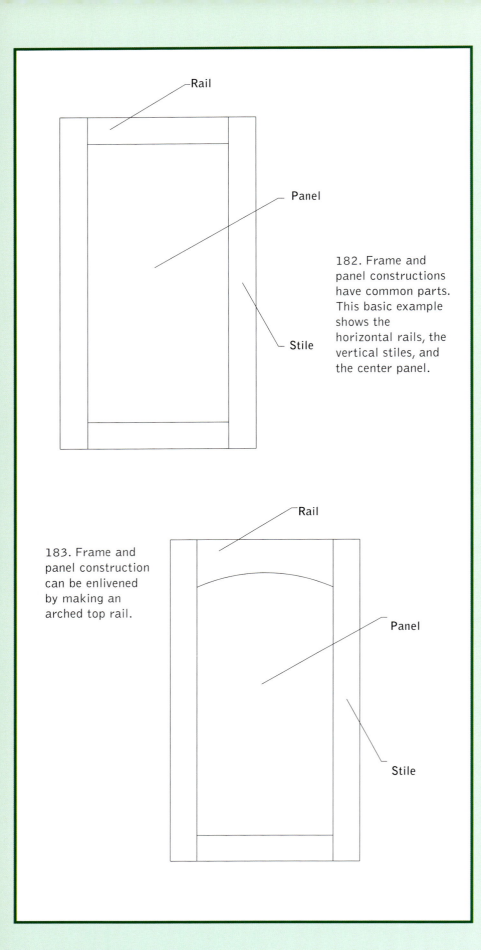

Rail

Panel

Stile

182. Frame and panel constructions have common parts. This basic example shows the horizontal rails, the vertical stiles, and the center panel.

183. Frame and panel construction can be enlivened by making an arched top rail.

Rail

Panel

Stile

Take a look at Figure 181. This is going to be a large, top-heavy piece. The installation is also unique and complex. Therefore, I've decided this mantel will be painted on-site after installation. Notice that the design calls for the pilasters to sit underneath the frieze rather than the frieze fitting between the pilasters, as in the Chapter 7 mantel. The pilasters are a raised panel construction with a two-piece base. The frieze is composed of a bottom cove moulding application below, two fluted header pieces above the pilaster, and a center raised panel with keystone detail. Topping off the frieze is a perimeter dentil trim. The cornice consists of an MDF routed top with 3-1/2-inch crown moulding below.

We'll start this project by milling all the solid-wood parts, including the pilaster and center frieze panel and frame, in addition to the various hardwood mouldings. Since this is a painted mantel, you could elect to out-source all of the solid wood mouldings. Most are available in local lumber yards as pre-primed moulding or compatible solid wood species. If you choose to use stock mouldings, design your mantel around the selected profiles. If making your own, the mantel design dictates the moulding profile. When milling solid wood, always add at least a 10% waste factor to the net quantity. This allows for the inevitable problems associated with milling solid lumber, including knots, twist and cupping, machining waste, etc.

Examine the nomenclature

drawing for frame and panel construction (Figure 182). The frame, like that on a picture, runs the perimeter of the construction and consists of four pieces in two categories: stiles and rails. The stiles are the vertical members. Most stiles are made the same width; typical dimensions range from 1-1/2 inch to 3 inches. The horizontal members are the rails. These can either be made the same width as the stiles, as in most cabinet doors, or varying widths to create visual interest. In addition, the rails can either be straight or arched (Figure 183). The panel is the piece in the center. The eye tends to focus on the panel detail, like studying a painting rather than its frame. The panel is set into a groove cut into the frame. Panels dictate the look, so it's important to know your options. Basically, you can have either a flat panel (Figure 184), or in the case of this mantel's pilaster design, a raised panel (Figure 185). Raised-panel construction requires panel thickness of 1/2 inch to 3/4 inch. This will be determined by the cutters you are using, and how much you want the panel to project from the face of the frame. For stain-grade work, the raised panel must be constructed of solid lumber because you are cutting into the wood, exposing its interior. On painted work, I often use MDF for the panel because it eliminates the tedious process of gluing up panels. On the other hand, flat-panel construction is much simpler. When incorporated in a 3/4-inch frame, the most typical panel thickness is 1/4 inch. At this thickness you must use manufactured veneer ply-

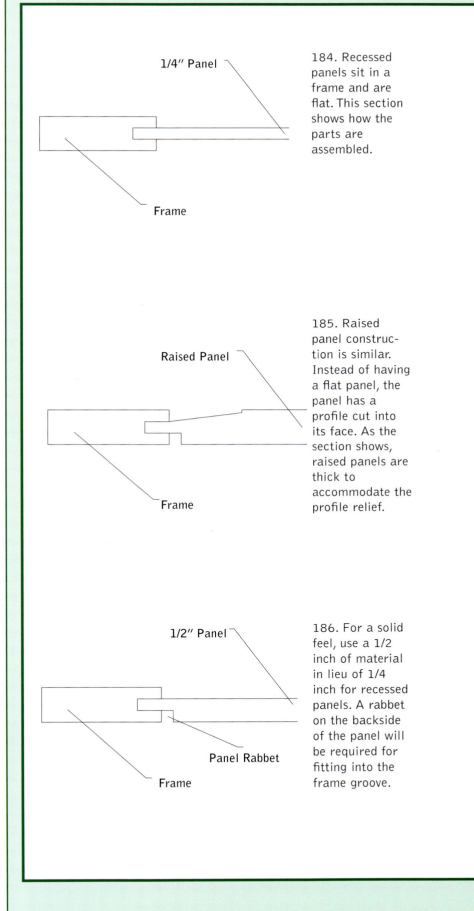

184. Recessed panels sit in a frame and are flat. This section shows how the parts are assembled.

185. Raised panel construction is similar. Instead of having a flat panel, the panel has a profile cut into its face. As the section shows, raised panels are thick to accommodate the profile relief.

186. For a solid feel, use a 1/2 inch of material in lieu of 1/4 inch for recessed panels. A rabbet on the backside of the panel will be required for fitting into the frame groove.

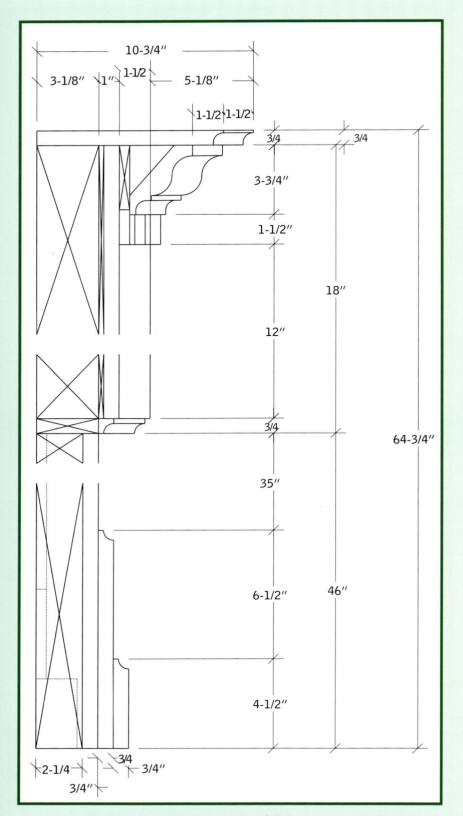

10-3/4"
3-1/8"   1"   1-1/2   5-1/8"
1-1/2 1-1/2
3/4   3/4
3-3/4"
1-1/2"
18"
12"
3/4
64-3/4"
35"
6-1/2"   46"
4-1/2"
2-1/4   3/4   3/4"
3/4"

187. The shop drawing section of the custom painted mantel project shows all the vertical dimensions. In addition, note how this drawing shows the center panel projecting out from the face of the end-fluted panel. This is a detail you could not determine by looking at the elevation alone.

wood for stain-grade work. MDF or veneer plywood is used for paint grade work. To create a more solid feel, use a 1/2-inch thick panel. The increased thickness does not deflect when pressed, nor does it change the frontal appearance. It will however require rabbeting the perimeter to fit in the standard 1/4-inch groove (Figure 186).

Dimension the stiles, rails, and return pieces from solid 4/4 poplar stock. Both stiles and rails are to be 2-1/4-inch wide. The return pieces for the pilasters are 3-1/8-inch wide. This is how far the pilaster projects from the wall (Figure 187). The center frieze projects 1-1/2-inch from the main frieze body. However, the returns are 2-1/2 inch to allow for the adjacent 1-inch thick fluted panels (as described below). Since the base is 11 inches high, the pilaster bottom will receive two separate rails instead of one large one. All solid wood is to be milled to 3/4-inch net thickness.

I purchase most lumber in the rough 4/4 dimension, which is a full 1 inch thick. Start by cutting your stock to rough lengths, determined by the material length you purchased, as well as the lengths required for the project. It is easier to handle short pieces, but prematurely cutting all stock at this stage is wasteful. I recommend leaving the pieces as long as you can. When you do cut rough lengths, leave a minimum 4 to 6 inches for final trimming. Next, joint one face (Figure 188), and then one edge (Figure 189). This gives you one 90 degree corner from which to make your pieces square. Take your wood to the table saw to dimension it to the rough width. Since you cannot rely on the table saw to give you clean cuts, rip the parts to the net width plus 1/8 inch. Ripping lumber on the table saw releases tension in the wood. This can result in a tapered or bowed cut straight from the saw. Allowing the extra 1/8 inch gives you the opportunity to plane the wood down to a consistent width and thickness. In addition, the planer cut is smooth and will require less sanding. At the planer, surface the lumber down 1/16 inch on each edge to achieve the net width first (Figure 190). Then, plane the lumber to the net 3/4-inch thickness. By preparing your stock in this manner, you end up with square stock that has clean, straight edges. Once all the solid lumber has been dimensioned, I run it through the drum sander (Figure 191). It's better to sand out defects and planer marks before making any profile cuts. Profiles can be damaged with early aggressive sanding. When coming straight from the planer, start with 80 grit for harder species and 120 grit with softer woods.

Next we shape all appropriate mouldings. The base receives a simple cove on the top. I've made this with a router table and power feeder (Figure 192). Make at least two passes for a cleaner cut. The first pass should remove the bulk of the negative profile. Since less material is being removed, the second pass puts less stress on the router. This allows the cutter to just kiss the surface, minimizing chatter marks. The frame and

188. Jointing the face of a board on the jointer is the first step in squaring the wood. Since your hands will be close to the blades, always use push sticks.

189. Once the face has been jointed flat, you are ready to joint the edge. Keeping the face tight against the fence ensures a true 90-degree and straight edge.

190. When one face of a board is flat, you are ready to plane the board to final thickness. Most single-head planers have the cutters on top, so the board is fed with the flat face down. Get in the habit of standing off to one side because wood sometimes shatters during planing.

191. Sanding parts before profiling decorative edges reduces the chance of damage to the profile. Drum sanders make quick work of a tedious task. They work much like a thickness planer except sandpaper is used in place of a cutter knife.

192. Shaping moulding with a router table is safe and easy. By incorporating a small power feeder, your accuracy and enjoyment will increase.

193. Cope and stick moulding, as shown here, is a common joint easily attained with a shaper or router. The stick is the female or grooved piece on the right and the cope is the male piece or tongue on the left.

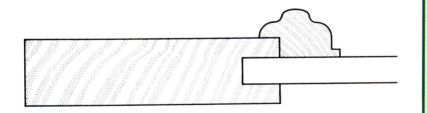

194. Applied mouldings can be included on standard frame and panel construction for more detail. Not only do they provide moulded interest, but also add greater depth to the panel.

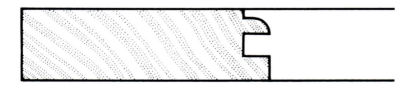

195. Cope and stick frames have the detail integrated into the frame itself. These must be produced either with a router or shaper.

panel design we're using has a cope and stick moulding profile. This refers to a construction method where similar moulding profiles have mating male and female parts that create a frame (Figure 193). This type of joinery commonly is found on both entry and cabinetry doors.

Note: A simpler form of frame and panel construction uses no moulding profile in the frame. Mating stiles and rails are joined together with either dowels or a simple mortise and tenon. If you don't have matching coping cutters, yet want the added detail, construct the frame with square stock and add a separate moulding piece after the frame and panel unit is assembled (Figure 194).

You need either a router or shaper to machine cope and stick profiles (Figure 195). Both shaper cutters and router bits are readily available to machine almost any desired profile. My setup is with a shaper. Set up the shaper with the proper height of the moulding profile (Figure 196). Next, adjust the in-feed and out-feed fences parallel and in line with the deepest cut on the shaper knife (Figure 197). By setting it up in this manner, the dimensions of your pieces will not change in width because you are only removing enough material to create the profile. If the in-feed fence was set deeper into the cutter than the out-feed fence, you would change the width dimension of your stock by the amount of the offset distance (Figure 198). Always double-check all your settings and make sure everything is firmly tightened down.

196. Setting up a shaper requires meticulous attention to detail. Start by setting the height of the cutter to the desired profile depth. Note the opening on the shaper table has been reduced to the smallest size possible for the cutter. This is a safety procedure that should always be followed.

197. Both the infeed and outfeed tables must be parallel to each other. First, using a straight edge, adjust the in-feed fence to the proper depth of cut in relation to the cutter. Next, place the straight-edge on the in-feed fence and adjust the outfeed fence so it is perfectly in line.

198. When the shaper infeed fence is set deeper into the cutter profile, the outfeed fence must be brought forward the distance of removed wood. It is imperative that the outfeed fence fully supports the material as it comes off the cutter.

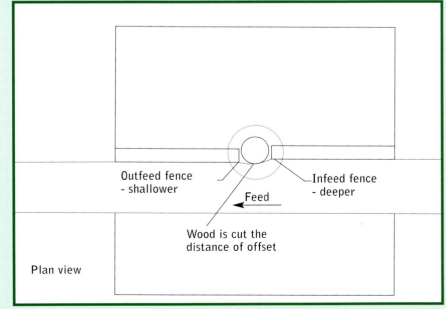

Outfeed fence - shallower

Infeed fence - deeper

Feed

Wood is cut the distance of offset

Plan view

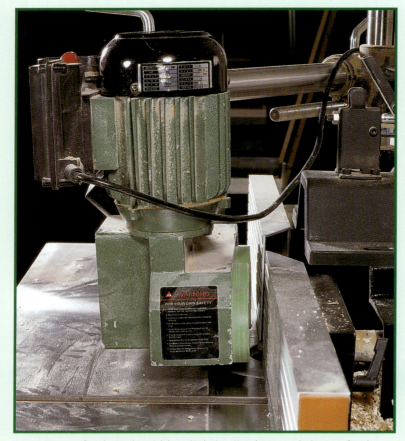

199. Power feeders should be slightly tilted toward the outfeed fence. This keeps the wood tight against the fence and prevents the wood from wandering.

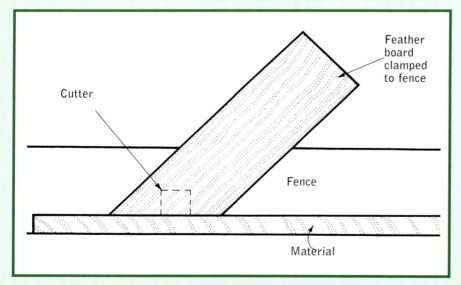

Cutter

Feather board clamped to fence

Fence

Material

200. A feather board or other hold-down device keeps material tight against the fence and cutter. This results in cleaner cuts, and allows you to keep hands at a safe distance.

Then, set the power feeder in place. Note how the feeder is slightly tilted toward the fence (Figure 199); this keeps your stock tight against the fence while preventing the board from wandering. You can perform this operation without a power feeder, but will need to install some additional hold-downs and cutter guards to protect yourself, and to achieve satisfactory results (Figure 200). A power feeder not only makes the operation much safer, but keeps an even pressure and feed rate, resulting in a more accurate profile and minimal or no burning. It is difficult to obtain consistent results by hand-feeding.

A note about running material through a shaper or router: The standard method of sending stock through a spinning cutter is to feed the material into the rotation of the cutter (Figure 201). This is the safest method because it keeps the control of the material in the operator's hands. Pressure is pushed into the operator's grip instead of away from it. The downside to this method is the greater tendency for the wood to tear out, resulting in damaged profiles. This is because the final cut is made as the cutter exits the wood. Tear-out can be greatly reduced if the material is fed with the direction of the cutter rotation instead of against it (Figure 202). However, this is an extremely dangerous operation and can ONLY be performed with a power feeder. Once the cutter comes in contact with wood being fed in the same direction, it wants to grab and throw the material. There is no way to safely protect

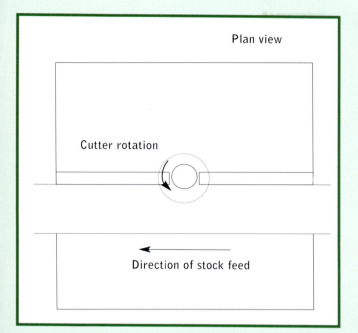

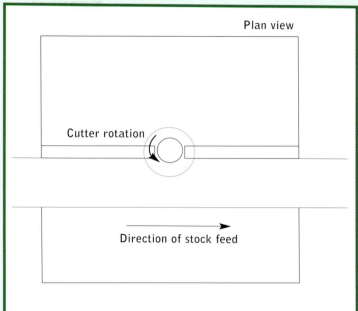

201. The standard and safest way to machine wood on a shaper is to feed the material against the direction of the cutter rotation. This method pulls the wood into the fence, leaving control in the operator's hands. Some tear-out can be expected.

202. For cleaner cuts with less tear-out, material is fed with the cutter rotation. However, this causes the wood to be pulled away from the operator. A **power feeder is the only way to prevent the wood from shooting out of control and must be used.**

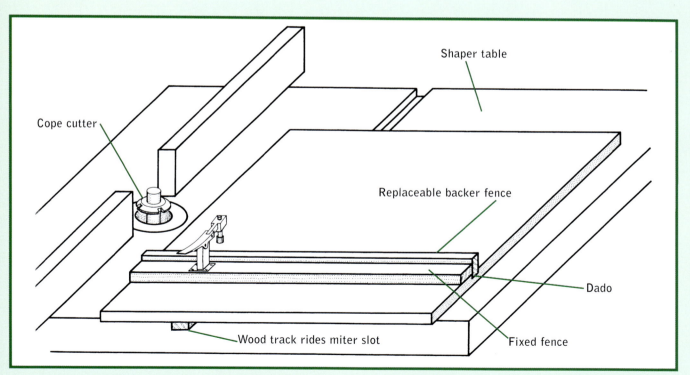

203 To help cut copes for frame-and-panel construction, build a simple shaper sled. It has a base and fence set at 90 degrees, and a toggle clamp for securing the work. A replaceable backer board helps reduce tearout.

204. Cut the stick profile as shown. Notice how the profiled edge is on the bottom, which means the cutter is on the bottom. Shaper cutters can be reversed so cutting can be done either on the top or bottom. Top-cutting not only leaves the cutter head fully exposed, but also requires perfect feeding pressure in order to cut accurately.

205. To set up the coping cutter, use a piece of the stick material as a gauge. This is the easiest way to achieve the correct height.

your body, the surrounding area, and even the material itself without the even, heavy force of a power feeder. If you plan on doing much shaper and router profiling work, the power feeder will give you safe, better results.

Always run a test piece through to verify that all settings are correct. Once you are satisfied with the test result, machine the decorative edge and groove into all the stile and rail material, including your 10% overage (Figure 204). Only the rails will receive the coped-edge profile on the end (described below).

Next, we cut the pieces to their final dimensions. The stile pieces are the height of the pilaster (46 inches) and the height of the frieze, not including the crown (12-1/4 inches). The rail pieces are the width of the pilaster (12 inches) and the center frieze panel (54 inches), minus the width of the two stiles (2 x 2-1/4 inch = 4-1/2 inch), plus the length of the two tongues (3/8 inch x 2 = 3/4 inch). This results in a net length of 8-1/4 inches for the pilaster rails, and 50-1/4 inches for the frieze panel rails. Now set up the shaper with the coping cutter for making the rail ends. Coping cutters have a center bearing that limits the depth of cut; this is critical for precise joinery. Use a piece of the profiled moulding to set the height of the coping cutter (Figure 205). Cut and run a test rail piece to verify both dimension and profile accuracy. Dry-fit the test rail.

To run the rail pieces, use a miter gauge to keep the wood perpendicular to the cutter (Figure

206). Make sure you have a wooden fence to back up the coped cut as it will greatly reduce tear-out. To enhance the miter gauge, construct a sled that allows the use of a hold-down clamp to secure the piece (Figure 203). After all the frame pieces are cut, and before you change the shaper settings, dry-fit both pilaster and frieze frames to ensure satisfactory joints.

As mentioned above, the panel that fits into the frame will have a raised panel profile. I construct this panel with MDF because of its stability and ease of fabrication. The net size of the pilaster panel will be the finished frame opening of 7-1/2 inch x 31 inch (Figure 207), plus the depth of two grooves (2 x 3/8 inch = 3/4 inch), minus 1/8 inch in both directions for wood movement. This gives a net pilaster panel size of 8-1/8 inch x 31-5/8 inch. The frieze panels are figured the same way, yet allow for the angled end by the keystone. The panel is to be 3/4-inch thick. The raised portion is cut on a shaper or router. The cutter can be set to shape either from the top or bottom. I prefer the cutter set on the bottom, that way the face of the panel is down when machining. This method is safer because the cutter is not exposed when machining. It also prevents snipe. This is when the panel inadvertently lifts into the cutter during the machining process. Snipe cuts are difficult to repair because they create irregularities in the depth of the profile (Figure 208). If pressure on the panel is not even when the cutter is positioned on top, sniping

206. Coping cutters have a bearing to control the depth of cut. Set both fences in line with the bearing. Using a miter gauge with a wood backer board, run the rail ends through to receive their coped cut.

207. Dry-assemble the frame parts to double check overall size. By measuring the opening size of the frame you can determine the net panel size.

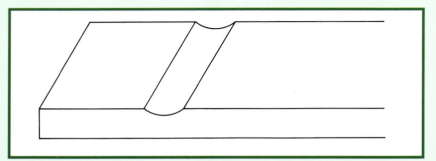

208. Snipes occur when wood lifts up into the planer or shaper head. If you are unable to adjust the infeed and outfeed rollers to prevent this, allow enough material to cut it off later.

209. Machine the raised panels on the shaper. For safety, make the cuts from the bottom. Use a sacrificial wood fence to reduce the amount of blade exposure.

210. Even with the raised profile cut on a 3/4-inch panel, it still won't fit into the 1/4-inch groove. A back-cut or cove is required to dimension the tongue to the needed 1/4-inch thickness.

will occur. Uneven panel pressure from a bottom-set cutter can be remedied by running the panel through a second time. Set up the power feeder and run a practice piece through first. Don't take all the material off with one pass; use at least two passes for cleaner work (Figure 209). With 3/4-inch stock for the panel, the back will need to be relieved so the panel fits into the 1/4-inch groove in the frame (Figure 210). I use a cove cutter to machine all four edges. This operation should be done after you have cut the front raised profile.

Note: When cutting a raised panel out of solid wood, machine the bevel across the grain on the first pass and work your way around the panel. This helps eliminate unwanted tear-out by cutting off the tear-out from each 211 cut (Figure 85).

With the panels cut, do one more dry assembly to detect potential problems. We're now ready to glue the assembly. With frame and panel construction, you only apply glue on the frame. The panel does not get glued in, it simply floats in the groove allowing it to move with seasonal changes of temperature and humidity. If it were to get glued in, the movement of the wood could either cause the panel itself to split or the frame joints to pop open. Spread glue on both the tongue and groove (Figure 212), being careful not to have excess glue squeezed into the panel groove. Clamp both rails, using a block of wood between the clamp and panel, and check for squareness. This is best achieved by measuring corner to

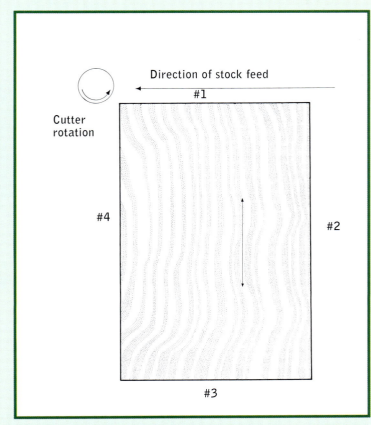

Cutter rotation

Direction of stock feed

#1

#4

#2

#3

211. To reduce the amount of tear-out when shaping a raised panel, begin with an end-grain side first. Work your way around the board as shown. Tear-out that occurs on the exiting cut on the end- grain side will be removed by the next cut on the long grain edge.

212. Put glue on the tongue of the rail and in the groove of the stile where the tongue will rest. You do not want glue to squeeze out into the groove, because the panel needs to float free in the groove.

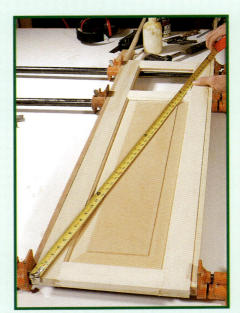

213. Check for square by measuring the diagonals. If the diagonal measurements are equal, the panel is square.

214. You can also use a large framing square. Check all corners and adjust the clamps until you're satisfied the panel is square.

215. Making sure the panel is square is not enough. Too much or uneven clamp pressure can cause the assembly to bow or twist. Place a straight edge along the face of the joint to ensure it is flat.

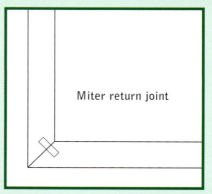

Miter return joint

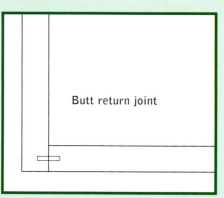

Butt return joint

216. Mitered joints eliminate the exposed joint line that butt joints expose. Whichever joint you use, a spline or biscuit should be included. This not only strengthens the joint but also makes it easier to align.

217. Cutting long miters is best done on the table saw. Tilt the blade to a 45-degree angle. Clamp a wood fence to the standard fence and raise the blade into the wood fence.

218. The object of the cut is to not change the dimension of the panel being mitered. Cut test pieces until the blade cuts right to the corner. Since no material is being removed from its face , the panel can still support itself on the outfeed side of the fence.

corner (Figure 213); equal corner dimensions mean a square panel. A framing square can also be used (Figure 214). Small brad nails are often used from the back to hold the panel in place without restricting its movement. Before leaving the assembly to dry, check to make sure the frame is flat at the joints (Figure 215). Uneven clamp pressure can cause buckling.

Once these have dried, sand the joints flush. I like to miter the return pieces, rather than using a butt joint (Figure 216). With a painted project, you need to eliminate as many visible joints as possible. Miters are ideal because they reveal no joint lines, only a corner. To cut the miters on a long board, I use the table saw. The panel was glued up first because it's very difficult to clamp a raised-panel pilaster with mitered edges. To cut this miter, set up the table saw with an auxiliary wood fence that the blade can cut into. Start by positioning the fence to a distance of 3/4 inch from the blade. With the blade set at 45 degrees and recessed into the saw table, turn the saw on and slowly raise the blade until it just cuts into the auxiliary fence (Figure 217). Run a test strip of your material into the blade to determine the cut location. The objective is to cut a miter on the piece without changing the dimension or width of the board (Figure 218). Fine tune your setting and run the mitered returns, pilaster panels, and center frieze panels through (Figure 219).

Cut biscuits or a through spline (Figure 220) to attach the returns. Set the biscuit cutter's fence to 45

219. Cutting the long miters on the panel is like ripping on the table saw, except the off-cut can get trapped between the fence and blade. To prevent kickback, stop the saw before the blade cuts all the way through. Remove the off-cut, then finish the miter.

220. Either a through spline or biscuits can be used to attach the returns. Never rely on nails and glue alone. Splines add strength and make alignment a snap.

221. When cutting biscuit slots for a miter joint, the tool's fence is set at a 45-degree angle. Keep the fence flat against the work surface or the slots may not line up.

222. Long miter joints require glue spread over the entire surface. Too much glue will prevent the pieces from joining tightly. Spread glue with a brush or small roller.

223. With biscuits and the mitered surface glued, you're ready to assemble. Line up the biscuits and press both pieces together.

224. Masking tape makes a great miter clamp. If your material was prepared properly, splines cut accurately, and the right amount of glue used, this may be all you need to hold the assembly while the joint dries.

225. Clamps are always a good choice for tightening up glue joints. Quick-action clamps like these speed up the process. The rubber contact points on the clamps protect the wood.

226. The glue-up is never complete until you check for square. Once the glue dries there is nothing you can do. A small try-square placed on the back of the miter tells the story.

227. Cutting the tabs on the stretcher can be done with a jigsaw or on the table saw. When using the table saw you risk over-cutting the notch since the radius of the blade will cut further into the bottom of the board than the top of the board. To limit the over-cut, raise the blade to maximum height, stop the cut short, and finish with a hand saw.

228. Predrill and countersink the screw holes through the stretcher and into the pilaster.

229. Apply glue to the joint and attach the two pieces together with wood screws.

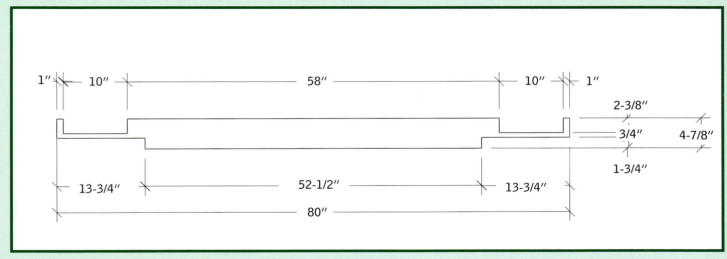

230. Here is the notching layout for the specialty plywood stretcher.

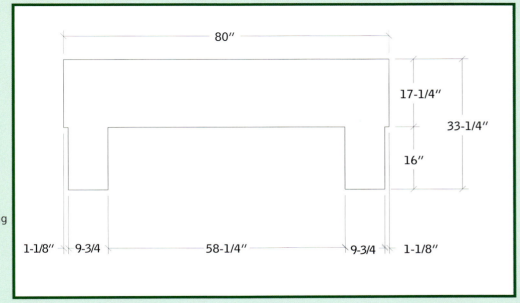

231. This is the tab cutting layout for the plywood skeleton frieze.

degrees. When cutting slots, make certain the fence of the cutter sits flat and parallel to the mitered edge (Figure 221). Use #10 biscuits for miters to lessen the chance of blowing a hole in the finished side. Run test pieces first to determine proper settings. Apply glue to the entire surface of the miter cut (Figure 222) and assemble (Figure 223). Use tape as a clamp to hold the joint. Too much glue will make it difficult to pull the miter tight. You know you have the right amount of glue when there is only a small amount of squeeze-out (Figure 224). If the tape is not providing enough pressure, use spring clamps, and as a last resort, quick-action or pipe clamps (Figure 225). Remember to always use a caul or block of wood between clamps and the finished work, unless you are using clamps with padded ends. Be sure to check for squareness before the glue dries (Figure 226). Sand when dry, in preparation for the base pieces.

Next, attach the two pilasters with a top stretcher. Only the bottom under the center frieze panel of this piece will be seen. For strength and ease of painting, I use a piece of 3/4-inch maple plywood. The stretcher acts as both the attachment for the 3/4-inch cove moulding (Figure 187, page 118) and the bottom of the center frieze panel. The length of the stretcher will equal the outside dimension of one pilaster to the other. Since the center frieze panel projects 1-1/2 inch from the face of the fluted panels (Figure 187,

232. After the crosscuts for the tabs have been made in the plywood skeleton, the rip cuts are made. By raising the blade to its full height into the plywood, the rip cut can be made, stopping 1 inch shy of the layout line.

233. To complete the tab cut, use a jigsaw or handsaw to cut into the corner.

234. With the pilaster and stretcher assembly turned upside down, the plywood frieze skeleton can be dropped into place.

235. The plywood skeleton holds the body together. A rigid connection of glue and screws is essential.

page 118), the stretcher needs to be cut with an additional 1-1/2 inch offset. Notch out the back of the stretcher where it attaches to the pilaster to allow for the plywood frieze skeleton, as described below (Figure 230). Leave a minimum of one inch at the ends of the stretcher when cutting the notch. Cut stretcher offsets either with the table saw (Figure 227) or jig saw. Glue, countersink (Figure 228), and screw the stretcher to both pilasters (Figure 229). Take care when turning the assembly over for the next step, as the plywood will remain fragile until the plywood skeleton frame is attached.

I use a plywood frame for the body of the frieze. Much like a skeleton, the plywood frame gives us the framework to easily attach additional blocking and decorative elements. This mantel will be embellished with the fluted MDF panels, and center frame and panel assembly. The skeleton should be flush to the outside pilaster dimension (80 inches) and reach the overall frieze height of 17-1/4 inch (Figure 187, page 118). To securely attach the skeleton frame to the pilasters, I've added an additional 16 inches to the height, which creates a tab that extends down into the pilaster. First, cut the skeleton frame to the overall size (33-1/4 inch x 80 inch). Then, layout the locations for cutting out the tabs (Figure 231). For a straight cut, use the table saw. When cutting on the table saw, the blade is wider where it comes out of the saw table than it is at the top of the material you are cutting. You must

236. Countersink the holes in the plywood stretcher. Attach the stretcher to the frieze skeleton with screws.

237. Use a framing square to check for square between the frieze and stretcher.

238. The finish frieze panel gets attached to the skeleton with a plywood blocking panel. Screw the blocking to the back of the frieze panel returns. A clamp holds the pieces tight while screwing.

239. Center the panel on the frieze skeleton. Use glue and screws to attach it together. Holes have been countersunk so they don't interfere with the next layer.

240. Staple 1/4-inch blocking on top of the 3/4-inch blocking. This will raise the fluted panels to the correct reveal height.

241. For added strength, attach blocking behind the frieze panel's top and bottom rails.

242. The raised panel frieze needs blocking to bring it up to the top of the frieze skeleton. This is then attached by screwing through the skeleton frame into the blocking.

allow for this so you don't over-cut the corner. For a 10-inch saw with the blade raised to its maximum height and cutting 3/4-inch material, there is about a 3/8-inch difference. Make the two crosscuts of the tab leg. Then, with the blade lowered into the table, set the saw fence to make the rip cut. Raise the blade into the wood to its maximum height and cut up to the tab cut, minus the 3/8 inch (Figure 232). Complete the cut with a jig saw to achieve a clean inside corner (Figure 233). With the pilaster assembly upside down, insert the plywood skeleton piece into the back channel of the pilaster legs (Figure 234). Leave the space that is the back of the pilasters open for field-applied blocking and easier fitting.

The frieze skeleton needs to be securely attached with glue and screws. First attach it to the pilasters (Figure 235). Next, glue and screw the skeleton to the plywood stretcher through counter-sunk holes (Figure 236); these will be filled before painting. Check for square between the frieze skeleton and pilasters (Figure 237).

The entire face of the frieze skeleton will be covered with the two 3/4-inch MDF fluted pieces and the center-raised panel assembly. First attach the center panels. Glue and screw 3/4-inch plywood blocking to the back of the panel assembly (Figure 238). Center the panel on the frieze skeleton and secure with glue and countersunk screws (Figure 239). Next add 1/4-inch blocking behind the location of the fluted flanker panels (Figure 240). This will allow the under-

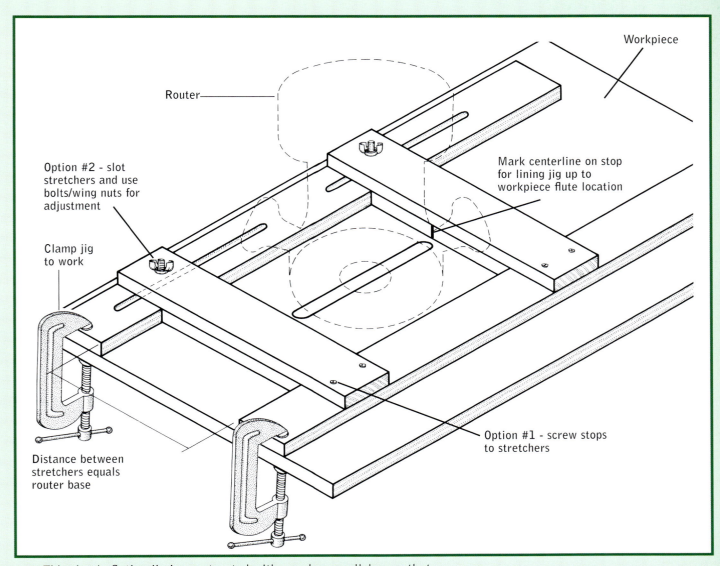

Router

Workpiece

Option #2 - slot stretchers and use bolts/wing nuts for adjustment

Clamp jig to work

Mark centerline on stop for lining jig up to workpiece flute location

Distance between stretchers equals router base

Option #1 - screw stops to stretchers

243. This simple fluting jig is constructed with wooden parallel arms that cradle the router. Stops at either end control the length of the flute.

244. Fluting with a router and a straight edge jig requires knowing your router base and center line dimensions. Measure the distance between the center of the router bit to the edge of the router base to find the centerline.

245. Routing flutes requires steady, deliberate movement to avoid chatter and burn marks. Plunge down to start the cut and don't hesitate until it's done.

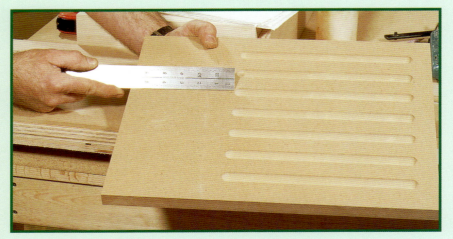

246. The flutes on our project stop 6 inches from the top of the panel to allow for the cornice moulding.

247. Since this mantel is going to be painted, I've elected to pin-nail the fluted piece from the front. With glue on the back, it only needs a couple of brads to hold it in place.

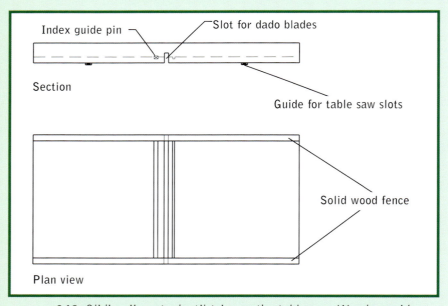

248. Sliding jig cuts dentil trim on the table saw. Wooden guides ride the saw's miter slot. Removeable index pins regulate the spacing of the dado cuts.

mounted 3/4-inch cove moulding to maintain its 1/4-inch setback from the face of the 3/4-inch fluted panel (Figure 187, page 118). You'll also need to provide blocking under the center-raised panel assembly at both the top and bottom (Figure 241). In addition, add blocking to the top portion of the center-raised panel, bringing it up to the top of the frieze skeleton (Figure 242).

The fluted faces overhang the pilasters by 1 inch on each side, for a net width of 14 inches. The height will extend to the top of the frieze skeleton. Cut both pieces to size along with the mitered returns. Now it's time to machine the flutes. A plunge router is imperative because it's the only way you can cleanly start and stop flutes. You'll need a jig to cut these accurately. I've got a commercial setup for cutting stopped flutes with a plunge router. You can also fabricate a wooden jig with stops for making the flutes. The simplest homemade jig is composed of two straight edges attached by two wood stops (Figure 243). The width of your router base will be the distance between the straight edges. Measure the center line distance of the router bit (or collet) and the edge of the base (Figure 244). Add this dimension to both the top and bottom of the flute length. This will be the dimension between stops along the straight edge. That same centerline dimension will also be used to line up the straight edge off the center point of the flute location. Make sure the jig is square to the cut and securely clamped down.

These flutes are 3/4-inch wide and spaced one inch apart from edge to edge, or 1-3/4 inch center line to center line. Since the fluted part of the frieze is 14 inches wide, we'll end up machining a total of seven flutes on each side. In addition, they'll stop one inch from the bottom and six inches from the top (Figure 246). The six inches allows room for the crown moulding on top. Run a test piece first to make certain your settings are correct. Start the router at one end, plunge down, and move the router with deliberate motion (Figure 245). If you hesitate, it's liable to burn the wood or cause chatter marks. If you've never attempted this before, try several test pieces to get the hang of it. When all flutes are cut, miter each end and biscuit together like we did with the pilaster legs. Remember, these panels have a right and left side! Attach the fluted panels to the frieze after the miter joints are dry. Use glue and either pin nails from the front, or screws from behind (Figure 247).

We are now ready to begin work on the cornice trim. First, there will be an accent piece of dentil trim. This will simply wrap around the perimeter of the frieze, creating the bottom of the cornice. The dentil trim measures 1/2-inch thick x 1-3/4-inch high (Figure 187, page 118). To create the dentil trim, machine and sand stock, if building a stain-grade mantel. For a painted project you can use 1/2-inch MDF. Make sure you sand the bottom edge prior to machining the dados. Spacing between cuts can be arranged however you

249. Make the dentil trim with a crosscut sled on the table saw. Make the first cut in the center of the trim.

250. After making the initial cut, insert the 1/2-inch indexing guide into the sled.

251. By placing a previous dado cut into the indexing guide, each successive dado cut can be made with consistent, even spacing. Work both sides of the initial cut until the dentil trim is completed. Firm pressure is required for good cuts.

252. The dentil trim sits 1 inch above the top flute to match the 1 inch spacing at the bottom. In addition, it needs to cover the joint between the raised panel frame and blocking by 1/4 inch.

253. With the cove moulding, work your way around the perimeter of the frieze bottom, pin-nailing every 8 inches.

254. Blocking needs to be applied above the dentil trim before the crown can be installed. Since it will all be concealed, the main concern is that it is the same thickness as the dentil trim.

like. I've chosen a simple 3/4-inch spacing with 1/2-inch w x 1/4-inch d cuts. You'll need to create an indexing guide to machine these accurately and efficiently. Making a crosscut sled for your table saw is a simple solution. Mine has two indexing bars that allows for making both 1/2-inch and 1/4-inch dado cut (Figure 248). To use the sled, place a stacked dado blade in the table saw to create the 1/2-inch width, and raise the blade the thickness of the sled (3/4 inch) plus the depth of the dentil cut (1/4 inch). I like to make my first cut approximately in the center of the board (Figure 249). Then insert the 1/2-inch indexing guide (Figure 250). Place the previously cut dado into the guide and effortlessly machine the remaining dados (Figure 251).

Before cutting the dentil trim, make certain you have centered it on the frieze panel, so you end up with equal reveals on both ends. The bottom of the dentil trim is one inch above the flutes and will overhang both the fluted panel and raised panel frame by 1/4 inch (Figure 252). Tape is a good clamp for outside miter corners. Cut, glue, and pin-nail the perimeter bottom-mount cove moulding (Figure 253). Prior to adding the crown, we need to nail blocking above the dentil trim (Figure 254). The blocking needs to be the same 1/2-inch thickness of the dentil trim, and the bottom should be sanded before attachment. We're now ready to move on to the centerpiece of the cornice: the crown moulding.

Crown moulding can be readily

255. Crown moulding can be produced with a shaper or router. The 3-inch cutter head on the left is designed for shaper work. The router bit on the right must be used in a router table. Tall router bits tend to vibrate, requiring extra sanding once milled.

256. Running a board through a moulder is the easiest solution for milling your own crown. This moulder accepts cutters up to 12 inches wide.

257. Several passes are required to make this 4-1/2-inch crown moulding. Here the freshly cut crown moulding passes under the feed roller and into the crown cutter knife.

258. In order to cut a 52-degree back bevel on a table saw that only tilts to 45 degrees, you'll need to construct a jig. Here the crown material rests on a sled with a 7-degree tilt. With the saw blade tilted at 45 degrees, you can cut the needed 52-degree back bevel.

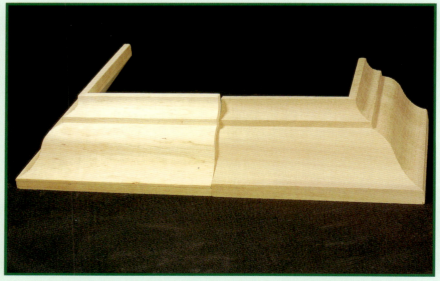

259. The crown on the left has back bevels of 52 degrees and 38 degrees. This set of angles is the most common and makes the crown moulding taller. On the left is crown that has two back bevels of 45 degrees. This set of angles shortens the moulding, but it projects out farther.

procured in a wide range of profiles and a limited number of wood species. For a paint-grade mantel like this, it only made sense to purchase the moulding. If however, you have chosen a peculiar pattern, species, or just can't seem to find what you want, it is fairly straightforward to mill yourself. The first option is to use a router. Single-piece crown moulding bits are available (photo 255), or you can run multiple patterns to create your own built-up cornice trim. Unless the single piece profile is less than two inches, I've found that the larger crown router bits leave too many chatter marks to sand out. The router also has the tendency to bog down when removing a lot of material.

A step above the router is the shaper. The shaper will better handle the larger profiles, so your options increase. In addition to standard profiles, if you have a moulding head, you can grind your own steel knives for custom profiles (Figure 255). If you plan to safely make good mouldings, then, as I stressed earlier, you must use a power feeder. Cutters larger than two inches are very dangerous and there is no safe way to effectively cut large mouldings without a power feeder. I use an old 12-inch moulder for making crown moulding. Knives up to 12 inches, or multiple knives, can be used in a machine like this.

Making the moulding is simple. Build an auxiliary table with guide rails that will hold the rough blank in place. Melamine works well because it allows the wood to slide smoothly. Prepare a rough blank of wood 1/4-inch wider than the profile, and for the crown, 3/4-inch thick. Adjust the moulder bed to take 1/16 inch of wood off with each pass (Figure 256). It takes about six passes to create the full crown profile (Figure 257). Next, cut the back bevels. This could be done either with another set of moulding knives or on the table saw. I prefer the saw because it's faster than setting up a new profile on the moulder. There are two sets of back bevel angles that determine how far the crown moulding projects from the wall (as described below). The 45-degree cuts are simple because it's just one setup of 45 degrees on the table saw. Make sure you cut the moulding with the profile or exposed side up. Cutting the combination angle crown requires a little more work initially. The 38-degree cut is a simple matter of setting the saw to 38 degrees and cutting as described above. For the 52-degree angle, you'll need to make an angled sled since the saw blade only tilts to 45 degrees (Figure 258). Cut a 7-degree back bevel for the sled board (45 degrees + 7 degrees = 52 degrees). Then attach a small stop block at the end to prevent it from sliding off the table as you cut. For cutting to length, crown moulding will require a compound miter cut for fitting corners. This is when you have two angles in different planes on the same cut. It's a very straightforward procedure if first, one understands the basics, and second, has access to a compound miter saw.

There are two basic ways the back bevel on crown moulding is manufactured. The first has the top

260. The crown moulding needs to be accurately located on the cornice. Make a pencil mark 1/4-inch below the transition joint of blocking and dentil trim.

261. If using a standard miter saw, small crown mouldings can be cut by placing them upside-down against the fence. Set the miter angle and cut the piece as shown.

262. Larger crown mouldings can be too big to set against the fence. Set the saw to the correct bevel and miter. Then place the crown flat on the saw table. Make the inside corner cuts first.

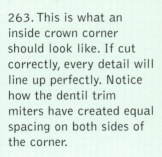

263. This is what an inside crown corner should look like. If cut correctly, every detail will line up perfectly. Notice how the dentil trim miters have created equal spacing on both sides of the corner.

264. By starting at the inside corner, it is easy to mark the location for the outside cut. Simply place the cut crown to the inside corner of the dentil trim and mark the outside corner on the crown. Notice the mark is placed on the bottom of the moulding.

265. Carry out the same procedure on the other end of the crown. The crown marked here will end up as a small piece. Notice how the piece being marked is large enough to safely handle while cutting.

266. The saw and material is now set up to cut the outside corner. To achieve good results, the work must be firmly held in place. Keep hand pressure down and back toward the fence, never toward the saw blade.

267. Attaching the inside corners is easier before nailing to the frieze. Apply glue to the ends and pin nail together.

268. With the crown indexed off the pencil marks, pin nail the partially assembled crown to the frieze.

269. Outside corners require extra attention because they are so visible. Take special care in alignment before nailing. Nail together the two pieces of crown together at the top and bottom before attaching to the frieze.

bevel at 38 degrees and the bottom bevel at 52 degrees. This set of angles is popular because it makes the crown moulding taller. The second method is with both bevels at 45 degrees, which shortens its height, but makes it project out farther (Figure 259).

Since the crown needs to conceal the joint between the dentil trim and blocking, make a mark 1/4 inch below the joint to index the crown (Figure 260). If the crown was small enough, the mitered cuts could be done on a standard miter saw. Turn the crown upside down and upright against the saw fence with the standard 90-degree bevel setting and 45-degree miter setting (Figure 261); this is considered a simple miter cut. Our crown is too large to set upright, so it must be cut laying flat using a compound miter. If your moulding has the 38- and 52-degree back bevels, the saw bevel needs to be set at 34 degrees and the miter at 31-1/2 degrees. If the crown has the two 45-degree back bevels, the saw bevel is set to 30 degrees and the miter set to 35 degrees. Once you have determined which back bevel crown you have, you're ready to cut. Start by cutting one end (Figure 262) from two crown pieces to create an inside corner (Figure 263). Hold the pieces tight in the corner and mark the location of the next cut (Figure 264, 265). Change the saw setting and in this case, cut the outside corner (Figure 266). Glue and nail together inside corners before attaching to the frieze (Figure 267). Pin-nail inside corners to the frieze (Figure 268). Outside

270. Even when the crown is nailed in place, the cornice work is still not complete. To prevent the moulding from sagging it needs additional support. Cut triangular-shaped blocks and glue into place every 8 inches or so.

271. Check if the crown is straight before proceeding. This is especially important with long runs and when using MDF mouldings, which have no grain structure to support themselves. Use a block plane to knock off any high spots.

272. Before the glue dries on the blocking, check to see that the face of the crown is straight as well. Add shims as needed.

The Cope Cut

There are two acceptable practices for cutting inside moulding corners: the miter and the cope cut. The miter, as described above, is the simplest method. When attaching moulding to square and rigid inside corners such as this mantel, the miter joint works fine. If attaching crown to an inside corner of a plaster wall, I recommend using the cope method. That way, when you cope an inside corner, the corner does not have to be perfectly square to achieve tight-fitting joints. The cope joint also does not open up as the building, and hence the moulding, moves over time. A miter joint will open up when not glued and nailed as described above. When coping an inside corner, run one side straight through to the wall with no mitered cuts. The coped piece is cut with the same compound miter you would use if mitering the joint. Then, back cut the material away from the revealed compound miter line (Figure 273). Place the piece against the previously attached crown (Figure 274) and drive it home. Although coping takes more practice, it is certainly the method of choice for field applications.

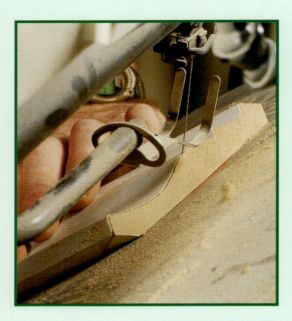

273. Making a coped cut requires removing the material behind the miter. Although usually done with a coping saw or grinder, in the shop I go to the jigsaw. When coping a joint, back-bevel the cope to remove material that may interfere with getting tight results. Notice how the jigsaw table is tilted to achieve that.

274. On the surface a completed coped cut looks like a miter joint. Notice how the attached piece on the bottom runs square to the end. The coped piece (above) has the mating piece profile cut into it. This creates a tight inside corner, even when the assembly is not a true 90 degrees.

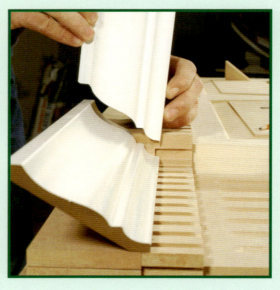

corners need special attention when aligning them (Figure 269). Be sure to add glue to the joint before nailing. I like to attach the crown as I go so each piece is indexed off its firmly attached mating piece. Work your way around the mantel until all pieces have been attached.

Next, we need to add some blocking to support the crown. It is essential to give the crown moulding a rigid base to rest on. Measure the distance of the triangle created behind the crown moulding. These dimensions become the base and height of the right-triangle blocking. Transpose these dimensions on 3/4-inch plywood and cut enough of these blocks to be spaced every 8 inches along the crown; use only glue at this time (Figure 270). With a straight edge, check the top of the crown to ensure it is straight (Figure 271). Use a block plane to flatten any high spots along the top of the crown that would prevent the shelf from sitting flat. Check the straightness of the face as well, adding shims where needed (Figure 272) before pin-nailing into place.

The final piece of the cornice to fabricate is the shelf. I've simplified its design by using a piece of MDF with a routed edge. This eliminates the need to attach a separate moulded profile. Measure the overall length of the attached crown moulding (Figure 275). To this dimension add 1-1/2 inch for each side (distance of shelf overhang) to give a net length of 92 inches. We calculate the depth with the same projection from the

275. Fabricating the cornice shelf starts with the dimensions. Measure the overall length of the crown moulding from outside corner to outside corner. Add the necessary overhang.

276. The cornice shelf has a stepped design, which will follow the way the frieze and crown step out from the pilasters. The cuts are made on the table saw with the blade raised to its maximum height. Cuts must be stopped shy of the inside corner to prevent over-cutting. The leading cut on a table saw is the material side that is facing down.

277. Finish the inside cut by hand. The advantage to using the table saw first is the straight cuts you get. Hand-cutting the inside corners is easy.

278. Cut the shelf front edge profile with a router. When cutting MDF, be sure to wear a dust mask. Notice how much airborne dust is generated.

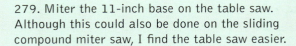

279. Miter the 11-inch base on the table saw. Although this could also be done on the sliding compound miter saw, I find the table saw easier.

280 Installed and painted, the mantel is complete. Designed as a mock mantel, it still conjures images of a warm fire. The baseboard used for the perimeter of the room also wraps the interor of the surround, creating the appearance of a slip.

crown and end up with 10-3/4 inches at the center section (Figure 187, page 118). The design calls for a stepped or notched shelf at the ends. First, cut the MDF at the 10-3/4- x 92-inch finished dimension. Lay out the notched section. Cut on the table saw (Figure 276) and finish the cut by hand (Figure 277) using the same procedure as described for the frieze skeleton. Sand the exposed edges to get rid of the saw marks. Now rout the profile on three sides. Because of the narrow width and stepped detail of the cornice shelf, I prefer to hand hold the router (Figure 278). Note that the profile is on the bottom side of the shelf.

The last piece to attach is the 11-inch base piece. For accuracy, miter the ends on the table saw (Figure 279), and glue and pin-nail only the face piece on the pilaster. As in the previous chapter, these returns will be field applied. The 4-1/2-inch base piece will be field-attached to allow for scribing to the floor. Now it's ready for installation! ●

281. Whether the finish is to be clear or opaque, preparation that includes hand-sanding is the key to fine results.

CHAPTER 9

Wood Finishing

Consider this chapter as a basic

introduction to finishing wood, with the intent of pointing you in the right direction. I'd like to break this discussion down into three main subjects: pre-finishing preparation, which will parallel the differences between natural wood finishing and paint preparation; natural wood finishes, which includes staining and clear coating; and opaque finishes, or what we commonly refer to as painting.

Ask any painter or finisher what the key is to a successful finish and he is liable to include preparation. This cannot be over-emphasized. Consider prep work like a builder thinks of laying a good foundation for a home: although not often considered when looking at the final product, it will certainly be noticed if it's poorly executed or ignored. Years ago I worked as a janitor for a large electronics company. Little did I realize at the time what valuable lessons I would learn while dumping trash and swabbing toilets. Most notably, people rarely make good comments when work is done properly, and always make comments when the work is done improperly. A pleasing finish appeals to the two senses of sight and touch and is guaranteed to elicit comments if the eyes and fingers do not approve. Remember, finishing is part of the fabrication process. A well-constructed mantel demands a quality finish in order to meet the criteria of the senses. Likewise, the same well-contrived piece can be ruined by a poor finishing job.

282. A random-orbit sander works great for general purpose sanding. These sanders have both circular and vibrating motions, which reduce the amount of scratches made by the sander. They can be fairly aggressive, so pay attention.

283. Nothing seems to beat old-fashioned hand sanding. For crisp outside corners, use a block of wood with sandpaper.

284. Finding scratches is not always that easy. By setting up a bright light to shine across the work (rather than from above), minute scratches can be detected.

WOOD PREPARATION

The first step in finish preparation is sanding the wood properly. Although you'll find many opinions on this subject, I think all can agree on the basic points I will make. Indentations caused by belt sanders, clamping, or mishaps, should be removed, particularly in painted projects where these divots (as a golfer would refer to them) will readily show up. Not always detectable through the eye, rely on your hands to find them. Close your eyes and run your hand across the work. It's surprising how much your fingers will "see" when not influenced by the eye. Cross-grain scratches also need to come out now or they'll leap to the forefront once the finish is applied. Use a random orbit sander on flat surfaces (Figure 282), and hand-sand mouldings and tight areas in successive grits, usually starting with 100 or 120 grit; use 80 grit if there are problematic areas. Finish up with 150 or 180 grit. All outside corners should be hand-sanded with a block (Figure 283) so you end up with a slightly eased edge. Not only is this more pleasing to the touch, but it also lessens the chance of damage from an electric sander. Some insist on sanding to 220 grit or finer, but I have found that to be unnecessary on mantel projects. Most of the surface is on a vertical plane, and the piece doesn't get handled like a door or table top. One thing to note: the finer grit you use, the more the wood grain will close. This may or may not be an issue when applying stain because the level of penetration could be affected. Between each grit, check your progress with your hand, feeling the surface for irregularities, and check visually. The best way to visually inspect your sanding prowess is by shining a light from the side rather than overhead. I blow the work off and use a halogen lamp (Figure 284). In this manner, the light is actually casting a shadow formed by the scratches and defects are more easily found.

Although fine cross-grain scratches are not as critical to remove in painted projects, don't be deceived into thinking you don't need to sand as much. You must sand thoroughly, with at least 150 grit on painted projects to eliminate visible scratches. Imperfections that only your hand can feel will be revealed to the eye after painting.

Painting intensifies imperfections because there is no grain to deceive the eye. Its uniform color and sheen reflect light in such a way as to reveal the areas you've neglected. A good rule of thumb to follow is: the higher the sheen (gloss), the more prep work you need to do. In addition, how the mantel is situated in relation to light sources such as windows, overhead lighting fixtures, etc., greatly affects what imperfections will be revealed.

Next, fill any cracks, open joints, or other imperfections with a matching color, sandable wood putty (Figure 284). This is the type of putty that hardens after a few minutes. When finishing a natural wood mantel, I usually leave nail holes unfilled until after finishing.

Sandpaper Basics

Abrasive Types:
- Garnet—A natural material, reddish brown in color. Softer than more modern abrasives, it wears out quickly, but leaves the smoothest finish of all abrasives.
- Aluminum Oxide—A synthetic material that is harder and more flexible than garnet. Probably the most popular and widely used woodworking abrasive.
- Silicone Carbide—Typically used for fine finishing. Can be used in both wet and dry sanding applications.

Abrasive Grain Coating Types:
- Open coat—Has space between the grains, which is best for rough sanding.
- Closed coat grains—Completely cover the adhesive and are used for semi-finish and finish sanding.

Crushing and Grading:
Mesh numbers designate the grade size. Particles that pass through a screen with 80 openings per square inch are called 80 grit. Those that pass through a screen with 120 openings per square inch are 120 grit, and are smaller. The larger the number, the finer the grit.

Backing:
Letters after the grit number designate the weight of the backing. There are four common weights:
- A—Light paper designed for light sanding operations.
- C, D—Intermediate papers with more strength and stiffness.
- E—Strong and very durable. Used primarily for drum and belt sanders.

285. Cracks and joints should be filled with a matching sandable type wood putty. Put just enough material in to fill, not overflow the imperfection.

Caulking

Caulking is a simple process. That could explain why you see so many poor caulking jobs. Sometimes when something appears so easy we end up doing a horrible job. Just a few notes to consider when caulking:

• Never use old caulk. Caulk gets hard and brittle with age. Fresh caulk is required for smooth joints.

• Purchase a "dripless" caulk gun (Figure 286). These only apply pressure when the trigger is squeezed, eliminating caulk leaking out when the gun is not in use.

• Cut as small a hole as possible at an angle in the caulking tube (Figure 287). Smaller holes allow better control of the caulking material. Larger holes are only recommended for filling large gaps.

• Invest in a caulking finisher (Figure 286). These inexpensive tools are great for cleaning up caulking joints. Once the material is put on with the gun, you can remove most of the excess with a clean, uniform line using the finisher.

• Putty knives are handy for cleaning out corners and small details. Remove all surface caulk. The only caulk that should remain is that which is in the joint you are sealing.

• Always have paper towels handy for wiping up excess caulk, and a damp rag to smooth out irregularities in the caulking.

• Proper technique includes forcing the caulking into the crack you are sealing. If you apply just a surface layer it will have a tendency to crack. Fill the joint with enough caulk to create a good seal.

• Caulking is better attempted after you have primed the work. The caulk adheres better to primer than raw wood, and all cracks will be more visible. If you must caulk before priming, take care to clean as much caulk off surrounding surfaces as possible. If not, lines of caulk will build up parallel to the joint and become very noticeable after painting.

286. "Dripless" type caulk guns release pressure on the contents immediately after letting go of the trigger, a material-saving and mess-reducing feature. At bottom left is a caulking finisher, a simple plastic corner tool designed to remove excess caulk.

287. For finish work, cut the nozzle at an angle and keep the hole as small as possible.

Sandable wood putties rarely stain the same color as the wood and only accentuate the nail locations. A better way to conceal them is to use color putty. Color putties are designed to be applied after the top coat finishing. They are available in both a crayon type form or in a container (Figure 288). Use the container type. It is soft, pliable, requires no sanding and can be mixed for good color matching. (Note: After filling holes with color putty, wipe the area off well with a clean rag to prevent smear marks on the finished wood.) Once the sandable wood putty is dry, sand thoroughly, and re-coat if shrinkage occurred.

If you are painting your mantel, all cracks, imperfections and nail holes should be filled before the final coat but after priming. This accomplishes two things. First, all areas to be filled are readily exposed. Second, caulking and spackle bond better to a primed surface than to raw wood.

Once you are satisfied with sanding, blow or vacuum off the surface dust (Figure 289). Use a tack cloth (available at most paint stores) and wipe the entire piece (Figure 290). Don't overlook this step. Tack cloths are designed to pick up surface material, and greatly enhance the finished product by eliminating dust particles. Use tack cloths after every coat of finish that has been sanded.

Painted mantels require even more insistent tack cloth use. Use the cloth before priming and after you have filled and sanded all holes and imperfections. Any top coats that get sanded will also ben-

288. Color putties are designed to be used after a piece has been finished. Use should be limited to nail holes and small imperfections. Available in crayon form or out of a can.

289. Before applying any finish, the wood must be cleaned off. Start by blowing the entire piece off with compressed air. Pay special attention to inside corners.

290. Blowing the dust off will not remove it all. Use a tack cloth to wipe the rest of the dust off. A standard rag will only smear the dust around, whereas a tack cloth will pick it up and remove it.

291. End grain accepts stain differently than edge or face grain. To help control the color, brush on glue. This reduces the amount of stain penetration, resulting in a more even finish.

292. The surface needs full coverage in order for the sealer to soak in and do its job, so generously apply the wood sealer with a rag or brush. Wipe thoroughly after five minutes.

efit from the tack cloth.

Note: Before using any finish, make sure you have an OSHA-approved organic respirator, as mentioned in the safety appendix. Breathing finishing fumes is not healthy. For $25 or so you can provide some inexpensive protection for your lungs. In addition, I recommend using industrial rubber gloves that won't dissolve with oil-based products, and painting coveralls to further protect your body.

SEALER

Before applying stain, the first step is to seal the wood. I use a product called Benite. Because it is a pre-stain sealer that seals prior to stain introduction, it provides better color uniformity. Generously apply the sealer, allowing it to penetrate the wood (Figure 292). After it has set for five minutes, wipe the wood thoroughly with a dry cloth, and allow to dry overnight. Pay special attention to the porous end grain. Stain wicks into end grain faster, making it darker than the rest of the wood. To prevent this, either apply several coats of sealer, or use glue sizing. Glue size is available as a pre-mixed product or you can make it yourself by diluting yellow glue with water. Brush it on the end grain (Figure 291), allow it to dry, and lightly sand. Sizing fills the open pores of the end grain so the stain does not penetrate as deeply, creating a uniform color, as on the rest of the wood.

After you have let the sealer dry overnight, you are ready to stain. I am assuming you have already tested the stain out on some sample pieces of wood. If not, stop right here and do so immediately! Do not apply stain on your project until you know it is the color you want.

STAIN

Natural wood finishes are characterized as finishes that allow the grain and texture of the wood to be seen. This can be enhanced with stain and is always treated with a clear top coat of some kind, such as penetrating oil, lacquer, varnish, polyurethane, etc. Stain not only brings out the depth of wood but also provides better color consistency throughout the piece. This is especially useful when mixing wood species. There are several different types of stain: lacquer-based, water aniline, and oil, to name a few.

Note: It is not uncommon to use both aniline and oil-based stains on the same project. For dark, deep colors I often use the aniline stain as the first coat for color depth. I apply oil stain as the second coat to enhance color clarity. As with any product, read the manufacturers recommendations for use and compatibility.

When working with oil stain and the color is different from what you want, generously apply paint thinner with a rag, rubbing aggressively to remove as much stain as possible. Although it will not remove all the stain, it will generally take enough of the color out so you can re-stain it to the hue you want.

Be generous when applying the stain to the surface. If you flood it to the point that a gnat would need scuba gear, you've applied too much stain. However, you do need to give the stain a chance to penetrate into the pores of the wood. Depending on manufacturer's recommendations, five minutes is usually adequate. If you wait too long, the stain will be hard to rub off and may not result in uniform color. Use a clean rag to wipe off the excess. If you rub aggressively, most of the surface stain will be removed. If you want the stain coat to be darker, either wait until the stain dries and apply a second coat, or don't rub as hard. A lighter touch on the rubbing process will leave more surface stain and require a longer drying time. Experiment on some sample stock before committing yourself. Most oil stains need to dry several hours, overnight is best, before applying the finish coat.

FILLERS

Wood like oak, ash, and mahogany is porous. Even after staining and applying the top coat the wood still has a textured look and feel. This effect can be reduced by using wood filler. Not required on closed-grained woods like maple and birch, paste wood fillers will fill the pores in the grain, resulting in a smoother finish to the touch. It is an extra step, and can be worth the effort if you are looking for a premium finish with these woods. Just a couple of notes on using paste wood fillers:

To use, thin the filler with mineral spirits or stain per manufacturer's recommendations. Apply liberally with a brush or rag, in the direction of the grain, working it

293. For better penetration and a smoother finish, oil finishes should be sanded while wet. Use 400 grit wet/dry sandpaper for good results. As always, sand with the grain.

294. Spray finishing is one of the quickest ways to get a professional quality finish. Use even, deliberate motion with the gun for consistent results. Notice the full body protection of the suit, facemask, and gloves.

into the pores. After it has set, usually in 15 minutes, wipe off all surplus filler with clean rags or burlap. Rub aggressively across the grain. To eliminate streaking, gently wipe with the grain. After the paste filler is completely dry, lightly sand the surface smooth. Use a tack cloth and you're ready for the top coat.

A note of caution: Whenever you use an oil-based product, always dispose of your rags properly. Rags must be spread outside to dry, or soaked in water until they are disposed of. Never leave oily rags in your house or shop; oily rags can cause spontaneous combustion and start a fire.

OIL FINISH

If you want a classic finish that doesn't draw attention to the top coat, opt for a penetrating oil. A good example would be tung oil, an easy-to-use product; simply brush or wipe the oil on. It takes the same basic procedure as applying stain: flood the surface, let it penetrate, and wipe off the excess. For better penetration and a smoother quality finish, use 400 grit wet-or dry-sandpaper to work the material into the wood before wiping the excess off (Figure 293). A minimum of three coats is typical. Other recommended oil finishes incorporate the water-resistant qualities of varnish. Daly's Profin is a good example. It can be brushed or wiped on. Simply apply a uniform coat, let it stand five minutes, and wipe the excess off. Apply a minimum of two or three coats, sanding with 220 grit or finer between coats.

Remember to use the tack cloth.

Oil finishes penetrate wood. This is why they need to sit on the surface before wiping off. These finishes allow wood to remain in its most natural-looking state. It will, however, require periodic maintenance of additional coats as the finish wears. Oil finishes are very easy to repair and maintain.

LACQUER FINISH

Much of today's millwork packages in residential construction involve the use of a lacquer top coat. It's easy to apply, dries fast and gives a good protective coating.

Lacquer finish sits on top of the wood as opposed to penetrating like an oil. Each successive coat bonds to the previous coat, making it easy to work with. This also allows the user to build up several coats on a piece to achieve the desired finish.

Available in different sheens of flat, satin, semi-gloss, and gloss, lacquer is an easy finish to use. The only requirement is that you have a spray unit (either conventional, airless, or high volume-low pressure) to apply it. Lacquer dries too fast for using a brush. If you have minimal skill in spraying, lacquer will become a personal favorite. The ease of use as well as quick drying time allows you to finish your mantel in just a couple of hours. There are different lacquer products available. Water-based lacquers, which take a little longer to dry, don't provide as clear of a finish, yet are less toxic to work with. Catalyzed lacquer is a modified nitrocellulose-based coating with an added catalyst that provides enhanced performance properties such as durability and water resistance. Standard lacquers, like their catalyzed cousin, are nitrocellulose-based but without a catalyst, which makes them less durable. Acrylic lacquers are "water white" in color, providing excellent non-yellowing properties.

Deciding which lacquer to use is up for debate. For the most protection, use a catalyzed lacquer. For finishes that are light in color, where yellowing would greatly alter its appearance, use a water-white acrylic lacquer.

Once the stain is completely dry, spray on the lacquer. This is best done in a spray booth or other well-ventilated area. You will need the best dust-free space possible. Cover over-spray areas with plastic, and use a tack cloth before spraying. Some lacquers require a sanding sealer coat, others are self-sealing. Check with your supplier. Spray with an even pattern, keeping the gun an equal distance from the wood (about eight inches) so you end up with a uniform coating (Figure 294). Be careful not to spray too much material on or it will run. After the first coat has dried (usually 30-60 minutes), sand with 220 grit or finer sandpaper. Use the tack cloth again and spray a minimum two or three more coats.

Many problems are associated with spraying finishes. A few worth noting along with the corresponding remedy are:

• Fisheye–Pin holes caused by an open pore or bubble rising in the finish or a contaminant in the finish. Check wood surfaces for contaminants and holes, then sand, and re-coat.

• Orange peel—Small bumps appear on the surface, caused by too much air at the nozzle, too little solvent, or over-spraying. Adjust spray pattern and solvent reduction (varies with coating manufacturer's specifications and type of spray unit you have).

• Blush—Whitish area on the surface caused by the presence of moisture in the finishing process. Check for moisture in spray line.

• Sags and runs—Caused by excessive coating thickness. Reduce the amount of time you spray each pass; scrape runs off, then sand and re-coat.

• Overspray—Caused when the spray from the front is pulled to the back by the exhaust system. Top coat needs to stay wet while all surfaces are coated.

• Dust and/ordirt—Caused by a dirty spray room, poor preparation. Clean area before spraying, and use a tack cloth.

VARNISH

Lacquers are an excellent option for mantels, because a mantel is not exposed to water or heavy handling. For a more durable finish, varnish and polyurethane provide better wear. Spar varnish is probably the most common. Because of its qualities, this finish has been around for many years. Designed to be brushed on, it will take a little longer than spraying. Tack-cloth the surface and use a good quality brush. Use even strokes for a bet-

ter looking final product. The biggest downside to spar varnish is its drying time: a minimum of eight hours. Make sure you finish this in a place that has minimal dust in the air. Plan on applying two coats.

Polyurethane has very similar qualities to varnish. Polyurethane is not quite as flexible as spar varnishes, but this is not an issue unless the product is used outdoors. Since mantels are typically classified as interior millwork (unless you are building one for your barbecue grill), it shouldn't matter. Do-it-yourself polyurethanes are generally brushed on, so the same application rules apply as for the spar varnish.

If you're set up to spray and you don't want to wait eight hours for your finish to dry, yet you need a finish more durable than lacquer, conversion varnish may be the answer. Conversion varnish employs the use of a catalyst, so it dries fast (30 to 60 minutes) and hard, and is an excellent option for the premium finish. Although slightly harder to work with, conversion varnish sprays and works very similar to lacquer. An important distinction to be aware of is its chemical properties: unlike lacquer, conversion varnish does not "weld" itself to the previous coat. It actually lies on top of the previous coat like a blanket. If I have too many blankets on the bed, I get hot and kick a few off to cool down. Conversion varnish feels the same way. Most manufacturers recommend no more than two coats over a vinyl sealer to achieve the proper mil thickness. Any more than that and you may discover the finish has cracked due to a hot night in bed!

"I want a premium, more durable finish. How do I decide?" Simple. If you don't have spray equipment, use brush-on polyurethane. With spray equipment, I highly recommend conversion varnish.

PAINTING

Preparing for painted millwork, as discussed in the preparation section, requires great attention to detail; so does the actual painting. Clear finishes are more forgiving because you see the grain of the wood through the finish. Opaque finishes, on the other hand, show you only the finish itself and every mistake you've made. The best beginning to a good paint job is the preparation. After that, it only requires patience and practice to get a good finish.

Again, there are a great many paint coatings available to use today: pigmented lacquers and varnish, latex and alkyd enamels, polyurethanes and epoxies, to name a few. Finishes such as opaque polyurethane and catalyzed epoxies are generally for professional use only. To achieve good results, they require skilled experience and a commercial finishing room.

First I'll touch on pigmented lacquers and conversion varnish; both have to be sprayed on. With the same basic qualities and characteristics as their clear cousins, application is generally the same. Pigmented lacquers are easy to use primarily because many coats can be applied. They develop a hard surface that resists damage. If they do get damaged, it is usually in the form of a corner or edge chipping off, making it difficult to repair just the damaged area. Overall, I would rate pigmented lacquers low on the durability list. They just don't hold up as well over time.

Conversion varnish is a much better finish, but harder to work with. Two top coats typically are all you can apply. It is much more temperamental than clear conversion varnish. If you don't have much experience or confidence, you may want to consider other options. Conversion varnish is not only tough and will withstand a lot of abuse, but has similar qualities to an automotive finish. Like lacquer, it is very difficult to touch up repairs.

"What is the determining factor on what type of opaque finish to use?" The best advice I can give is to determine your skill level. Lacquer is easy to spray, dries fast, but is the least durable. Conversion varnish provides an excellent quality finish but requires more skill. Enamels, as described below, are generally the most user-friendly. Although softer than lacquer and varnish, they are more resistent to abrasions and are easier to touch up. They also rate high in durability.

Enamels have become one of my favorite opaque finishes. They are available as latex (water-based), alkyd (oil-based), and quick-dry oil enamels. Latex enamels are good for wall surfaces. Many claim they equal oil-based paint for millwork. I disagree. The

Finish Equipment

The three basic types of finishing equipment are:

1. Conventional: This is the oldest and most basic. It uses a cup gun attached to a hose and air compressor.

2. Airless: This type uses a pump that moves the material through a hose. Material is usually used straight from the can and does not require thinning. Airless systems apply the most finish, the fastest. Great for opaque paints because of its ability to spray heavier materials.

3. HVLP or high volume low pressure: This system has a high volume of air generated by a turbine that attaches to a cup gun. HVLP systems produce the least over-spray and fine finishes. The material, however, must be thinned down more than usual to achieve good results.

brushing qualities are far superior in oil paints, since the paint has better flowing qualities. This means the paint is allowed to be worked longer, enabling more even coats and diminished brush marks. Latex paints dry faster and tend to leave more brush marks because of this lack of flow. In addition, many painted millwork packages are constructed of MDF, which does not like water. Latex paints are thinned with water. Water will raise the fibers in MDF, preventing a smooth, flat finish. An oil-based primer is mandatory. Even when latex paints are applied over an oil-based primer, the finish quality is not as good (at least as currently manufactured). Oil-based paints eliminate these concerns.

There are two types of oil enamel paints I will discuss: quick-dry enamel and standard alkyd enamel. Quick-dry enamel, as the name implies, dries fast. Under proper conditions it will be dry to the touch in under 30 minutes, and is a viable option when speed is a concern. It can be re-coated in two hours. Some claim its durability is less than standard alkyd enamels. Because it dries fast, it must be sprayed – don't even consider brushing it. Prepare the mantel surface as described above. Two coats over a good primer should be adequate. If sanding is required after the first coat, don't forget to use the tack cloth. Quick-dry enamels are slightly more difficult to work with than standard enamels because they dry so fast. This also means that touching up damaged parts is more difficult. Practice on sample pieces first!

Alkyd enamel is one of the best all-around opaque finishes available. It is certainly the most user-friendly. It can be brushed or sprayed. The finish coating is softer than varnish, which results in more resilience to damage. For instance, if a hard object strikes the surface, enamel will generally bend into the indentation. Varnish and lacquer on the other hand, may resist the impact blow all together, or, if damage does occur, it will be in the form of a chip coming off. This quality, coupled with the workability of the material, makes alkyd enamels the easiest of all to touch up damaged areas. Through the years I have conducted an informal survey among residential painters and finishers as to their favorite finish. The overwhelming response was alkyd enamels. This is also a popular choice among commercial finishers, even though they often use more technical finishes like polyurethane, epoxies, and polyesters. For a high quality, easy-to-work-with paint (both brushing and spraying), Benjamin Moore's Impervo is a good choice.

I recommend that if you can spray, do! You will end up with a smoother finish. However, if you can't, brushing will obtain very acceptable results. When painting with alkyd enamel, be certain you have a dust-free environment. It takes several hours to dry and you don't need dust settling in on your hard work. Don't forget to use an organic mask—these fumes are not pleasant. If spraying, use the same basic techniques as described for spraying clear coats. Spray evenly to get uniform coverage. If using an airless sprayer you should be able to use the paint as it comes from the can. My system is an HVLP (high volume low pressure). HVLPs do not move the material out of the gun as well, so the paint has to be thinned down to help it atomize better. Sometimes you'll need to thin beyond manufacturer's recommendations. Just don't thin the material so much that it sprays clear! Thinning will largely be determined by the type of equipment you are using. If you're not sure, call the manufacturer's representative, and don't be afraid to experiment. When brushing, use the material straight from the can. Make certain you use a quality brush designed for oil-based paint. If you find you do need to thin the paint, use a product like Penetrol. It thins the paint, allowing it to flow out better than if you use paint thinner. If you follow the basic painting principles of spray technique, material preparation, good spraying environment, etc., you won't have a problem.

Two coats of alkyd enamel over a good quality primer are recommended. This will provide you with a surface that will wear well for many years. ●

295. The cornice shelf is the last item to install. For a truly built-in look, the shelf needs to be scribed to fit tightly to the wall. With the shelf touching the wall at the high point and an equal overhang in the front, draw a scribe line on the shelf top following the wall contour.

CHAPTER 10

Mantel Installation

Completion of the shop work leads to an air of excitement. After going through the design process and building the mantel, your focus quickly shifts to finalizing the project, with the objective of placing the mantel in its final resting place. Don't however, let this excitement get in the way of common sense. Safe delivery to the job site, even if it's from your garage to the living room upstairs, is critical. The last thing you want is damage due to carelessness.

When moving a finished mantel from my shop to the job site, I take deliberate steps to avoid mishap. Most of my projects are built in sections, or component parts. This makes delivery and installation easier because the pieces are smaller and more manageable. However, since mantels are best pre-assembled in the shop, they are quite awkward during transport. The combination of size (often 6 feet w x 5 feet h) and the fact that it is a finished piece of millwork make it challenging to deliver safely. Although wood mantels are not usually very heavy (weighing on average a hundred pounds), their awkward shape can be cumbersome. Hence, the construction methods you employ require careful planning for installation as well as design.

Repairing Damage

An old cabinet maker once told me: "A good cabinet maker is not one who never makes mistakes, but one who knows how to fix them when they happen." Very good advice. Being a young woodworking disciple at the time, I was struck by the fact that he said, ".....when you make a mistake..." That is the first hurdle to overcome when working with wood, knowing that mistakes will come, and how to repair or alter them so the mishap is not apparent.

Dealing with scratches, dents, and holes on a pre-painted mantel means filling the problem area with appropriate spackle or filler, sanding flat, priming, and re-painting. For clear finishes, first determine if the scratch is in the finish only or down to the wood. If it's only in the finish, lightly sand out the scratch with 180 or 220 grit sandpaper. Re-coat with the appropriate finish. If the scratch went down to the wood, follow the steps outlined below. When sanding out a defect in a stained piece, you will often have to sand a larger area than the defect, so you can blend in the patch. Blending in stain can be tricky. To get a good match, you may have to experiment.

Here are some common mistakes and defects and how to fix them:

● Mistake/defect: **Scratches**
Gouges in the wood caused by a hard object or by sanding across the grain. **Remedy:**
Sand with successive grits, with the grain.

● Mistake/defect: **Deep scratches**
Caused by a hard object under pressure being pulled along the wood.
Remedy:
If unable to sand out, veneer over the scratch with matching wood.

● Mistake/defect: **Stress cracks**
A result of excessive clamping or other pressure usually around a joint.
Remedy:
Pull the wood apart without breaking any fibers. Work glue into the crack and re-clamp (Figure 296).

● Mistake/defect: **Common crack**
Naturally occurring, or a joint that didn't glue tight.
Remedy:
Wood putty can be used but is noticeable. For a better repair, cut a piece of veneer the length of the defect and flatten it with a hammer. Force glue into the crack and tap in the veneer (Figure 297). Sand when dry.

● Mistake/defect: **Dents**
Caused by a hard object striking the wood surface.
Remedy:
Moisten the dent with water, then use a heated iron to swell the wood fibers, forcing the wood to lift the dent out (Figure 298).

● Mistake/defect: **Knots**
A natural defect in the wood.
Remedy:
Fill with epoxy if the knot itself is not objectionable (Figure 299). Or, drill the knot out. Cut a plug of matching wood to the same diameter hole, glue, and plug (Figure 300).

● Mistake/defect: **Holes**
A natural or human-induced crack or hole in the wood.
Remedy:
Fill with matching wood putty, or make your own. Place a couple drops of super glue or epoxy over the crack, sand with fine paper, forcing the sawdust into the glue and crack.

● Mistake/defect: **Veneer bubble**
Veneer lifting off the substrate caused by inadequate glue or clamping pressure.
Remedy:
Slice bubble open with a sharp blade, inject yellow glue into the slit and re-clamp.

The first thing to do (if you haven't done so already), is to apply cross bracing to connect the pilaster bottoms as discussed in Chapter 7. I cannot over emphasize the importance of this step. Several years ago, I built a paint-grade mantel constructed entirely of medium density fiberboard. It consisted of an arched, raised panel frieze with raised panel pilasters. Truly a piece any artisan would be proud of. While moving it around in the shop without cross bracing and a carefully attentive mind, it fell to the floor and broke in half! I think I suffered mental anguish more severe than that poor mantel experienced. Although the cross bracing wouldn't have prevented it from falling to the floor, it certainly would have lessened the degree of damage. By adding one or more temporary stretchers (or bracing), you will be able to move the mantel around with more confidence. Since that mishap, I've been much more aware of the dangers of mantel box transportation.

If the mantel is pre-finished, take extra time to properly prepare it for moving before it leaves the shop. If you are simply moving it from your garage shop to the living room, this won't be as critical. Nonetheless, it is always a good idea to provide added protection. The majority of damage that I've seen is usually a result of poor preparation, rather than careless handling. When I move a mantel, I wrap the entire unit with packing material, typically foam sheets. To attach the foam I use 3-inch stretch wrap. Stretch wrap has no

adhesive that can damage finished surfaces. In addition, it pulls the foam tightly and provides additional protection on outside corners. If you must use tape, use a good quality masking tape and try not to let the adhesive side of the tape come in contact with the finished wood. Pay special attention to outside corners, particularly those of crown moulding. If not well protected, these will often be the first parts that get damaged. Remember, you can never be too careful at this stage! If transporting a mantel in an open-bed truck, wrap the mantel with visqueen plastic after the packing material is in place. This will give added protection against the open road hazards of dust, rain, and road rage.

For smaller jobs, I use my pickup truck to deliver a mantel. Since mantels are usually larger than the bed itself, I use the truck bed sides as a cradle to hold the mantel in place (Figure 301). First, lay blankets underneath the wood contact points. Place the pilaster feet on one side and the frieze on the other. This provides adequate support to prevent racking. If the height of the mantel is not long enough to safely span the distance, use enough padding and/or blocking to safely support the piece. After positioning it carefully in the bed, lay additional moving blankets over the top of the mantel. Securely tie the unit down, making sure you have adequate anti-chafing material where the rope comes in contact with the mantel. You don't want the rope pressure burning a groove in a corner of your finished product.

301. Although wider than the bed of the truck, a mantel can be safely transported with a standard pick-up. With the mantel carefully wrapped, lay the assembly flat on top of the bed rails. Securely fasten with rope or straps.

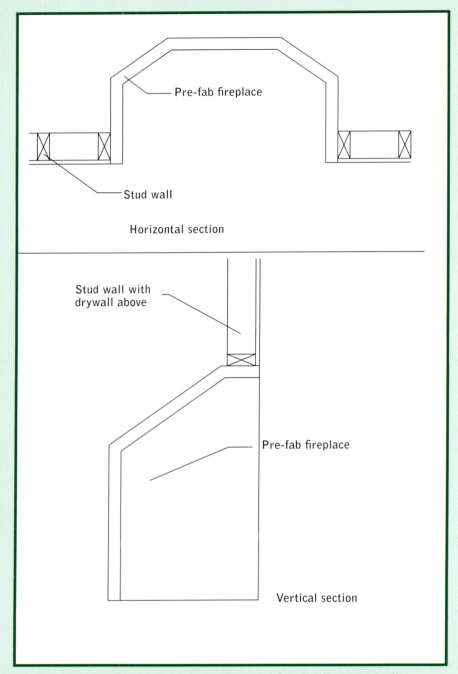

Pre-fab fireplace

Stud wall

Horizontal section

Stud wall with drywall above

Pre-fab fireplace

Vertical section

302. Pre-fabricated or manufactured fireplaces are typically installed in a wood-framed opening. This type of construction makes mantel installation easy. All parts can be attached directly to the wood studs.

Once at the job site, it's time to jam! By now your adrenaline will be pumping. All the preparation in design and the fabrication work in the shop is about to be realized through this final step. This is where you find out just how well you measured the conditions. You'll also discover whether the design you chose meshes with the room's other architectural elements. The anticipation of seeing all this come together can create a bit of anxiety. That's why you will usually be very motivated during the installation procedure. In fact, I have to be careful not to drink too much coffee at this stage of the job. Excitement can be a good thing, but it must be tamed. Mistakes often result from an undisciplined mind.

From the initial site analysis, you should have a good idea of the path to take into the house. This may seem a trivial step, but I've worked in houses that had many options to choose from. Do I take the path through the front door by the Dale Chihuly glass work, or around the back, up the stairs on the new handsewn European carpet? Any items that would be better moved or covered, do so now. Regrets are a result of something you should or could have done. Think it through beforehand and you won't have any. Once the path is clear, get an extra set of hands and move the unit to its new home. Have a spot in the room cleared where you can place the mantel at a safe distance while you prepare the fireplace opening to receive it. If I can't find a safe spot to lean it up against, I'll lay the mantel down flat on the floor. By doing this I know I can eliminate a repeat of the arched mantel mishap in my shop. It was embarrassing enough being alone at the time. Can you imagine being in someone else's home performing that kind of show for them? That would be a tale told over and over, much like a good movie or joke!

Lay a drop cloth around the area you're working in. Materials and tools can then be placed without fear of damage to the flooring (remember our discussion about regrets?), Typically, most mantel installations require very little, if any, demolition work. As described in the fabrication Chapters 7 and 8, the nailing cleat is all you will need to attach the mantel to the wall. This will either be a flat piece of blocking that the mantel attaches to, a French cleat, or panel clip as described later.

If you are installing millwork around a prefabricated fireplace unit (i.e., zero clearance), there will be wood framing members you can screw to. This is because the prefabricated fireplace units are self-contained. Their basic construction includes a specially insulated metal firebox and a chimney pipe that allows wood framing members to be placed right up to the face of the shroud. Prefabricated fireplaces are a modern fireplace construction method. This means the framing and wallboard around them will most typically be drywall (Figure 302). A comparable situation would be a fireplace with masonry located on the exterior of the house. These are framed very similar to the pre-fabricated

type, with the wood framing members located close to the firebox area. With this type of fireplace construction, providing blocking for your mantel is easy. Simply locate the wood with a stud finder (Figure 303), and mark out where the blocking needs to sit with level (horizontal) and plumb (vertical) lines. Then screw the blocking (3/4 plywood or solid wood pieces) through the drywall into the studs. If there is no wood or metal framing whatsoever behind the drywall, you'll need to add some blocking. Cut a section of drywall out. Locate the nearest framing material and attach a piece of blocking to it. When performing this operation on a finished wall, I've found that screws are much easier to control than nails. Screws pull the wood together well without disturbing the finished drywall. Nails, on the other hand, push the wood apart and cause vibration to the surrounding wall. Patch the drywall joint and install the mantel another day.

If there is framing material that you can drive at least two screws into from different locations, the remedy is much easier. The first choice would be to use a hollow wall anchor. There are many types available. Look for one that spreads out behind the drywall. This type will provide better support. Drill a hole through the wood blocking for the hollow wall bolt. Mark the anchor location in the drywall by holding the blocking in place on the wall. Then, drill through the wallboard for the anchor. Insert the screw through

303. Pre-fabricated fireplaces will have wood framing surrounding the metal firebox. Use a stud finder to locate the wood members.

304. Hollow-wall anchors require predrilling all holes. Here, the hollow-wall anchor has already been threaded into the blocking. Notice the predrilled hole in the drywall that the bolt is being fed into.

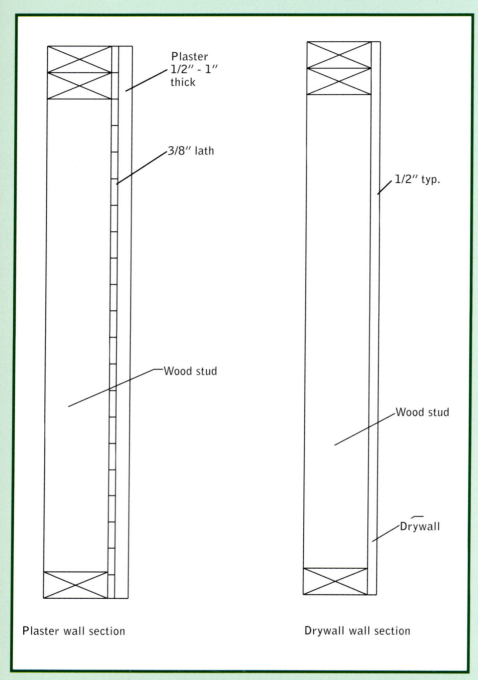

Plaster
1/2" - 1"
thick

3/8" lath

1/2" typ.

Wood stud

Wood stud

Drywall

Plaster wall section

Drywall wall section

305. Wood lath and plaster walls are commonly found in homes built before the 1950s. Modifying this type of wall can be tricky since the plaster tends to crumble around the cut lath. By the 1960s, drywall had become the method of choice for interior walls. Its single sheet construction makes modifications a breeze.

the blocking hole and attach the wing nut. Squirt some construction adhesive on the blocking and line the bolts up with the drywall holes (Figure 304). Tighten down the anchor and you're set.

Another solution is to simply squirt construction adhesive onto the cleat and screw to the drywall, taking care not to spin the screw once it's set. This should provide enough support since you already have a couple of screws in the stud. In addition, the weight of the mantel is distributed to the floor by means of the pilaster legs. If, however, the mantel is very top heavy, or does not extend to the floor, or you want to provide adequate earthquake insurance, you will need to add blocking behind the drywall as discussed.

If working on an older home where the mantel comes in contact with the wall surface, you may have to deal with plaster instead of drywall. Plaster walls are a little more difficult and messier to work with. If there are adequate framing members behind the plaster, the procedure would be the same as described above. If you need to attach a couple of hollow wall anchors, installation will require more attention to detail. Plaster is held on the wall by plaster lath. In the old days, lath boards were used that measured 3/8-inch thick x 1-1/2-inch wide, spaced about 1/4-inch apart (Figure 305). As the plaster is applied, it pushes into the spacing and acts as an anchor to the wall. Plaster by itself will not support anything, so if you drill into that 1/4-inch spacing cavity, the plaster will crumble. Putting a

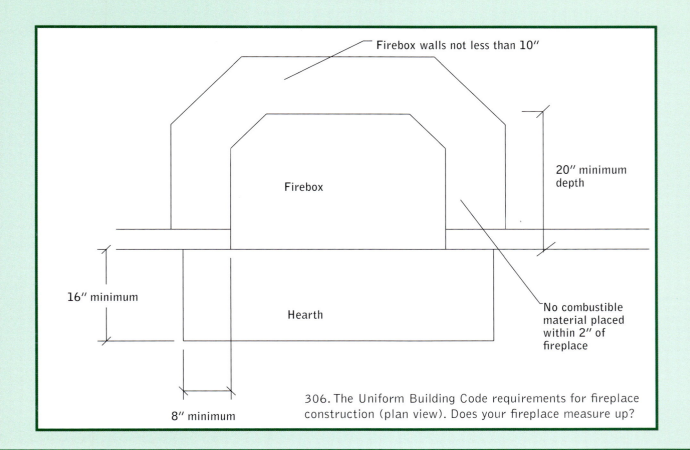

Firebox walls not less than 10"

Firebox

20" minimum depth

16" minimum

Hearth

No combustible material placed within 2" of fireplace

8" minimum

306. The Uniform Building Code requirements for fireplace construction (plan view). Does your fireplace measure up?

screw right into the wood lath often causes the wood to split and the plaster to crumble. To avoid this, pre-drill all holes carefully. Both hollow wall anchors and the adhesive/screw method will work in plaster, just be careful.

Standard masonry fireplaces require more attention when attaching blocking. First, the inner masonry provides the fireproof envelope. Hence, no combustible material can come in contact with this fireproof envelope, which is the firebox or smoke chamber. Study the drawing above (Figure 306).

The Uniform Building Code

- Section 3707-c: Fireplace walls to be not less than 8 inches thick and firebox walls to be not less than 10 inches in thickness, except where a lining of firebrick is used, those walls cannot be less than 8 inches.

Fireboxes shall be not less than 20 inches in depth. Joints in firebrick shall not exceed 1/4 inch.

- Section 3707-h: Combustible materials shall not be placed within 2 inches of the fireplace, smoke chamber, or chimney walls.

- Section 3707- l: Hearths shall extend at least 16 inches from the front of, and at least 8 inches beyond each side of, the fireplace opening. Where the fireplace opening is 6 feet square or larger, the hearth extension shall extend at least 20 inches in front of, and at least 12 inches beyond each side of, the fireplace opening.

Depending on how the building was framed and the fireplace built, these clearance dimensions could have been increased even further beyond where you need to attach the blocking. In some cases, they may have even framed the walls less than the two-inch clearance

requirement. It is now your responsibility to discover what was done before proceeding. When the Uniform Building Code specifies the two-inch clearance, they are talking about the space between the fireplace, smoke chamber, or chimney walls. Understand that the code is referring to the masonry portion that contains the fire. This does not include brick veneer that is applied as a decorative element. Brick veneer is essentially a separate wall, not part of the fireproof envelope. Because it is a non-combustible material, it typically goes right up to the firebox opening and deceives us into thinking we cannot attach directly to it. It is therefore important that you understand what you can and cannot attach your blocking to. Once you have determined it is a deco-

307. Two basic types of masonry fasteners to use are Tapcon screws, as shown on the left, and lead anchors on the right. A hammer drill with a carbide-tipped drill bit is required for consistent, frustration-free drilling.

308. Set the mantel into place for prefitting. If everything lines up, you're good to make it secure.

309. By leaving the mantel shelf off, you're able to easily secure the mantel to the wall. Drive screws through the plywood blocking and wall at the stud locations. Keep the level handy during attachment.

310. Since the base returns were left off in the shop, screwing the pilaster bottom to the blocking is easy. Countersunk holes will prevent the screw heads from interfering with the applied base. Nails would work too, but adjustments are more difficult.

311. A nail or two along the pilaster leg helps pull the surround tightly to the wall.

rative veneer only, follow the guidelines outlined in Chapter 2 regarding distance from firebox opening (UBC section 3707-h). Check with your local building department regarding local codes.

Your finished mantel is like a piece of furniture: any attachments should be concealed and unobtrusive. The two basic masonry fastener types to choose from are lead anchors and Tapcon screws (Figure 307) as described below. First, cut the wood blocking to the required length. Then predrill holes in the wood blocking a minimum 12 inches on center. Then, hold the blocking up to the layout lines and mark the hole locations onto the brick by hammering a nail through the blocking holes. Lead anchors require all the anchors to be in place before attaching the wood. A specific hole size is required for each type of anchor depending on its use. For this application, a 1/4-inch anchor is adequate. This will require a 1/4-inch hole to be drilled in the masonry. A standard drill with a masonry bit will work, but it's worth purchasing or renting a hammer drill for this operation. A hammer drill adds a pulsating or hammer-type action to the circular motion of the drill. This added feature makes drilling masonry almost as easy as drilling through wood. After all the holes are drilled, tap the lead anchors in place. Next, apply construction adhesive to the back of the wood blocking and screw it into place.

The other masonry fasteners, Tapcon screws, are much simpler to use. These are specially designed to go directly into the masonry without an anchor. They provide all the necessary holding power you'll need. Available in many sizes, I use the 3/16 x 2-inch screws. The procedure here is a little different. Pre-drill all the required holes in the wood, not more than 12 inches on center, with a standard 3/16-inch bit. Don't use the carbide bit for the wood, it causes pre-mature wear to the bit. Hold the blocking in the desired spot on the masonry wall and mark the fastener locations with the masonry bit in the drill. Drill the masonry hole. Apply construction adhesive to the board, plumb, and tighten the screw securely. Then drill the rest of the masonry holes at once. Insert the remaining screws and you're done. Plan your holes to go into the masonry brick itself instead of the mortar; the brick will give better holding power. In addition to being faster, the Tapcon method doesn't require pre-drilling the masonry holes prior to wood attachment. A word of caution: don't be tempted to unscrew and re-screw the Tapcon screw anchor. The first time into the masonry hole the threads tap the hole and bite down. When unscrewed, the masonry has the tendency to crumble, unlike wood, which has more resilience.

Once you have all the cleats secured, set the mantel in place for pre-fitting (Figure 308). Check for level and squareness at the firebox opening. Don't forget to make sure the mantel is centered on the opening. If not, it can wreak havoc on the appearance of the finished stone work. Shim if necessary. When everything looks good, you're ready to attach the mantel. With the top shelf off, you can easily attach the mantel with screws from above since this will be concealed by the cornice shelf (Figure 309). Drive three to four screws into the blocking or wall framing material. Now concentrate on attaching the pilasters. I prefer using screws whenever possible. If you have to make any adjustments, the screw can easily be backed out. They are harder to conceal, however, and may not be practical. Finish screws are the best choice because the head is smaller than a standard screw. With the base off, you can screw directly through the pilaster bottom. Simply countersink the heads to prevent interference when the base gets attached (Figure 310). Two screws into each base are more than enough. Once I'm happy with the placement at this point, I'm comfortable using nails. If I must, I'll drive a couple of finish nails, either by hand or with a pneumatic gun, into the blocking where the pilaster meets the wall (Figure 311). These will either be covered up by scribe moulding (providing you keep them back far enough) or filled with color putty.

Now, cut and attach the return sides of the crown moulding and base. Since I recommended precutting, sanding, and finishing this mitered piece in the shop, you may want to use a scrap piece to ensure you get the proper dimension. Walls can be deceiving and you may find that the required cut is not square. Once your cut pieces

312. Cut the return crown pieces to fit tightly to the wall. Add some glue to the miter joint and pin nail with 18-gauge brads.

313. Complete the process with the pilaster base returns. Outside miters should be glued and nailed first, before attaching the return to the pilaster leg.

314. With the pilaster base returns in place, the room baseboard can be reinstalled. The base is cut to die into the pilaster leg. Finally, the 1/2-inch x 3/4-inch baseshoe that runs the entire perimeter of the room is wrapped around the pilaster plinth block.

fit snugly, glue the joint, and tack nail it with 18-gauge brad nails (Figure 312). Continue the process with the mantel base returns (Figure 313). Attach necessary room base where it meets the pilasters (Figure 314) and then you can get off your knees.

Next, you'll put on the mantel shelf. Set it in place and see how it fits to the wall. You want to achieve a gap tolerance of no more than 1/16 inch from the back of the shelf to the wall. If the gap is greater, you'll need to scribe the top. If you made good templates prior to fabrication, you could have pre-scribed the shelf in the shop. This is nice to do when practical because it saves time during installation. Scribing, or cutting the material to fit the wall, can be achieved with many different tools. For larger scribes a jigsaw works great. Always cut from the underneath side. You do this for two reasons. First, you don't risk the chance of the base scratching the finish. Second, jigsaws cut on the pull stroke. If you cut from the bottom, the blade cuts into the finished side toward the back, eliminating tear-out. For finer scribing a belt or disc sander can be used. My preferred choice is a 4-1/2-inch disc sander. It provides fast material removal and easy maneuverability. It takes practice to get good at it, so take it slow.

To lay out the scribe line, set the top in its location, pressing it tightly against the wall. Next, measure the overhang distance in the front and on the sides. Adjust the shelf until it has the same overhang dimension on all three sides.

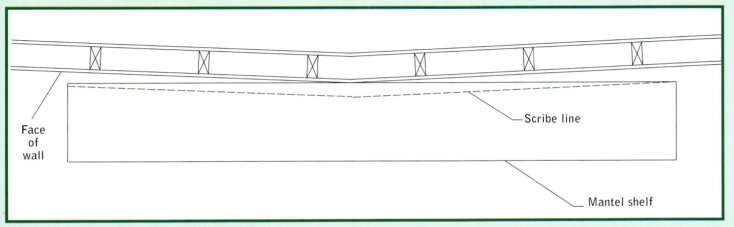

Face
of
wall

Scribe line

Mantel shelf

315. When scribing a cornice shelf to the wall, place the shelf with equal distance off the front of the mantel, and touching the wall at the bow. Using a scriber or compass, transfer the contour of the wall onto the shelf for trimming.

316. The cornice shelf is the last item to install. For a truly built-in look, the shelf needs to be scribed to fit tightly to the wall. With the shelf touching the wall at the high point and an equal overhang in the front, draw a scribe line on the shelf top following the wall contour.

317. With a properly scribed shelf, the plasterboard wall looks perfectly straight. A small amount of caulk in the remaining seam eliminates the dark shadow line.

Equal side overhang ensures the top is centered. Equal overhang in the front assures you that your scribe line will keep the shelf parallel to the front crown moulding. Now check the gap in the back along the wall. The largest gap you have on top is the amount you need to cut or scribe. For instance, if you have a 1/4-inch gap on the left side, you need to cut or scribe the 1/4 inch off the right side (Figure 315). Since the walls are rarely flat and even, unless masonry, it

may vary in dimension all the way across the top. To make your scribe layout line, take a scriber and set it to the largest gap dimension. I usually just hold a pencil and let my finger act as the scriber. Then move the scribe, keeping it tight against the wall, along the entire distance of the top (Figure 316); this is the line you cut to.

After you are satisfied with the scribe cut (Figure 317), you are ready to attach the cornice shelf. If you have any pencil lines left over

from scribing, take the time to remove them now as it's easier than dealing with it after it gets installed. If you have to caulk the gap later, the pencil line will become even more pronounced. I like to glue the top on with the minimal amount of nails. Using construction adhesive, run a generous bead around the perimeter of the cornice crown. Just be careful not to put so much on that it oozes out onto the finished portion. Place the shelf on top. If pos-

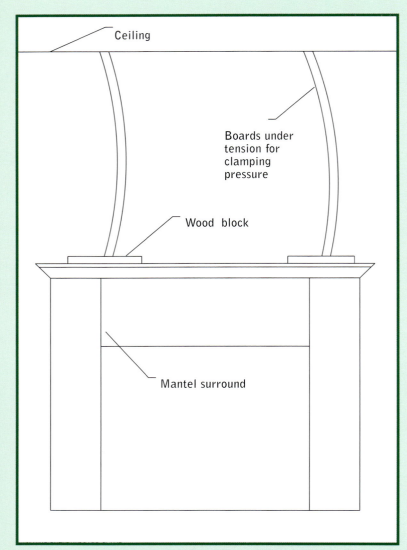

Ceiling

Boards under
tension for
clamping
pressure

Wood block

Mantel surround

318. Braces under tension against the ceiling can be
used to glue a cornice shelf into place. This eliminates
the need for a mechanical fastener. This maneuver is
particularly handy when installing pre-painted shelves.

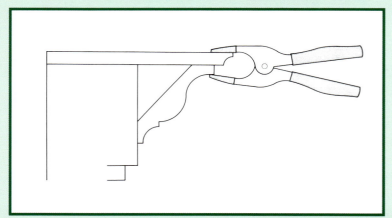

319. Spring clamps are great tools to use to field glue
cornice mouldings to the shelf. If nail holes are
objectionable, you've got to plan a way to secure the
pieces together before fabricating the mantel.

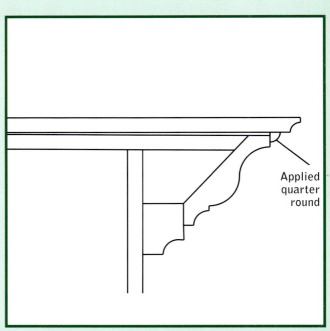

Applied
quarter
round

320. If gaps do appear at the crown/shelf
transition, a small quarter round or other
moulding profile can be used. Sometimes this is
desirable to produce more detail.

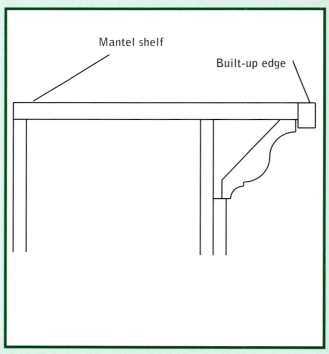

Mantel shelf

Built-up edge

321. Mantel shelves can also be constructed
with a built-up edge. The advantage of this
method is that you eliminate the exposed field
joint between the shelf and cornice trim.

sible wedge it into place with boards positioned from the ceiling to the shelf (Figure 318). If the ceiling is too high, a couple of spring clamps might work (Figure 319). In a pinch, I'll drive a couple of inconspicuous pin nails in the back. It just needs to hold until the glue dries. This works fine if you have a natural wood mantel or one that will be painted on site. If the mantel was pre-painted in the shop, any nails you drive while in the field will require repainting. Driving nails through a pre-painted mantel should be your absolute last option. If you are unable to pull the shelf down tightly enough to the crown, a small quarter round or other trim can be installed after the shelf is in place (Figure 320). This is one way to eliminate gaps generated on site. The mantel in the installation photos used another approach to shelf design: a built-up edge (Figure 321). This is the easiest way to conceal inconsistencies in field-installed shelves.

Gaps between the wall and pilaster can be filled in three ways: scribe the pilaster, use scribe moulding, or caulk. Perhaps the cleanest look is achieved by scribing the pilaster. Although it's a basic procedure, it is more difficult. Scribing means you handle the mantel unit more, increasing the chance of damage, especially when a lot of scribing is needed. If the wall has severe bumps in it and you're sold on this method, consider scribing the piece prior to pilaster assembly. This requires you to template the wall area first, and scribe the pilaster returns in the shop. An easier and more common procedure is to use scribe moulding. Since the moulding is a smaller dimension than the pilaster leg, it will bend and flex to the contour of the wall. Simply cut your piece to the proper height, apply pressure toward the pilaster and wall, and nail it into the pilaster. The scribe moulding's biggest drawback is the surface holes the nails leave after attachment. If the mantel is painted, you'll need to repaint, as described below.

The third way to fill a gap is by caulking. Don't ever rely on caulk for gaps wider than 1/16 inch. Although it will span the distance comfortably up to 1/4 inch, it becomes very noticeable beyond 1/16 inch. Caulking should be a finishing touch, not a replacement for scribing. Natural wood mantels don't always require caulk to look finished; in some applications they look better without. Painted mantels, on the other hand, always require caulking at the scribe points (in addition to every other joint, as discussed in Chapter 9).

When all the pieces have been attached, it's time for the finishing touches. All nail holes will need to be filled. For natural wood mantels, use color putty that matches the color of the wood. As mentioned in chapter 9, the pliable color putty works better. You can easily custom mix the color to match. It also cooperates better than the crayon type when forced into a hole. After filling the holes, don't forget to rub well with a soft cloth. If you neglect this step, the excess putty that smeared around

322. Panel clips are designed for hanging panels, mantel surrounds, and any other piece where a concealed fastener is desired. Shown here is a manufactured aluminum clip. One clip gets attached to the work; the other clip mounts to the wall. If multiple pieces are being hung, use longer lengths of the extrusion on the wall rather than the short 3-inch clip.

323. French cleats are another form of concealed fastener. These are easily fabricated from plywood mitered on the table saw.

the hole will become visible after several weeks. And it's harder to remove later. Painted mantels require all holes to be filled with a spackling compound. Spackle is applied first, allowed to dry, sanded, and filled again if needed. All field-applied moulding joints on a painted mantel will need to be caulked, as well as all scribe points at the wall. Cut the opening on the caulk tube as small as possible to minimize the flow. Fill the gaps completely. Next, you'll want to remove the excess caulk to form a clean 90-degree angle. If you use a caulk finisher, this will remove the bulk of the bead without causing excessive smearing. Finally, use a damp cloth to smooth out the bead even further. Apply additional caulk if needed.

After the caulk has dried on your painted mantel, you're ready to paint. So long as you have only nailed through the scribe mouldings, the field painting will be easy. Since field applied mouldings sit in different planes, cutting a clean paint line is a snap. A pre-painted mantel should never have to be painted again on site. Only the field applied mouldings should. If the design demands more painting than the field moulding, or the installation is awkward and complex, consider painting the entire unit on site instead.

If you chose to attach the mantel shelf, crown, and base ends in the shop with the intention of installing the unit as a totally prefinished product with no field-applied scribe mouldings, you'll need a concealed fastener that won't puncture the finished product. For this I recommend using French cleats. These are mating hanger pieces that work much like a coat hook. Gravity holds the piece in place. They can be purchased in the form of aluminum panel clips (Figure 322), or made with plywood cut to a 30-degree bevel (Figure 323). The French cleat provides a means of attachment without surface fasteners. If you can design your mantel this way, I highly recommend it. As long as the walls are straight and flat, the installation will be very fast.

The French cleat will have to be attached both to the fireplace wall and the back of the mantel. The piece that attaches to the mantel is positioned as far back as the thickness of the cleat from the mantel back. Its mating piece will attach directly to the wall. Measure the proper horizontal location and draw a level line. Place the cleat in position and secure it to the wall. Then it's a simple matter of lifting the mantel over the cleat and dropping it into the locking cleat position. For added rigidity against house and earthquake movement, put construction adhesive on the mating portion of the cleats, and/or a couple of screws at the base.

If you set the mantel prior to any finished stone work, you dictate where the stone will go. If, however, you put the mantel up after the stone, make sure the stone is in place before you fabricate the mantel, especially if someone else is responsible for the stone work. If not, the tile setter may make a carte blanche deci-sion about size or some other detail that effects the way the mantel is installed. The last thing you want to encounter during installation is an obstacle that could have easily been resolved before fabrication. ●

324. Kitchen designs are taking advantage of the mantel's popularity. When placed over the cooking area, these mantel hybrids are reminiscent of the days when people prepared food in their fireplace.

CHAPTER 11
Specialty Features

I'M OFTEN CALLED UPON TO FABRICATE a mantel that incorporates shelving, entertainment centers, or other forms of woodwork into the mantel's design. Rooms with fireplace walls often lend themselves to this. The key is good planning. Knowing beforehand that you want cabinets or other millwork on the same wall will go a long way in making the project easier to plan. Putting a mantel on a wall with integrated cabinetry will typically be the last step in such a project. Consider other millwork as the undergarment, and the mantel as the outer garment that overlays adjoining millwork. You must make the necessary allowances on the adjoining millwork for the mantel, not the other way around.

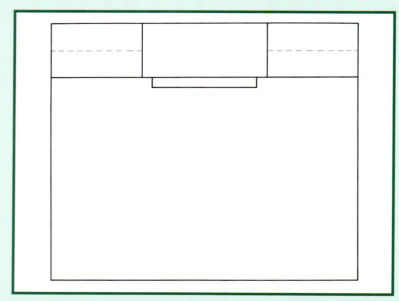

325. With a recessed wall by the fireplace, cabinets can be built flush to the fireplace front. The beauty of this application is increased millwork, storage and minimal intrusion to the room.

326. This elegant setting pairs a white painted mantel with a dark green marble slip and hearth. Built-in cabinetry flanks both sides of the fireplace, extending the mantel's reach. Above the cabinetry on each end are lighted display areas that further enhance the setting.

327. Maple pilaster columns are the leading feature of this mantel. With matching maple cabinets, the eye scans the entire wall rather than focusing on the mantel surround. Recessed into alcoves, the cabinets reduce the projection of the fireplace.

CABINETRY

When incorporating a mantel on a wall with cabinets, the deciding design factor is how the wall is configured. Existing buildings typically don't offer a choice of wall configurations. Therefore, you need to be aware of how the different layouts affect design. If the wall recesses behind the fireplace opening, the cabinetry can be fabricated flush to the back side of the mantel (Figure 325). This creates a look that accentuates the mantel. The cabinetry is tucked behind, allowing the mantel to project and become the focal point. The face of the cabinets becomes the new wall. With this design, the cabinets do not encroach upon the space, but rather define it. The mantel in Figure 326 exemplifies this principle. The cabinets become part of the mantel. They are identified as cabinets, but the eye defines the millwork as a mantel first. This layout gives you the most flexibility with mantel design. With a recessed wall, you're not limited by what the cabinetry needs are. To be functional, a cabinet has minimal depth requirements. With a recessed wall alcove, those needs are usually satisfied without sacrificing floor space or encroachment on the mantel surround. In this situation, the mantel can actually be designed independently of the cabinets. It can either stand alone (Figure 327) or be incorporated into the cabinets themselves.

When the wall is flush or nearly flush to the fireplace opening, any cabinetry added will need to project beyond the face of the mantel (Figure 328). In this application, cabinets have a tendency to be the focal point. How much depends on how far they project from the wall. If you put in deep base cabinets, they will grab more attention from the mantel. Even narrow cabinets create a pocket or hole that the mantel falls into (Figure 329). When combined with functional cabinetry, the mantel can act as a bridge between components (Figure 330). Although the cabinets draw attention from the mantel, the purpose of the mantel is not lost, just redirected.

Planning for cabinets around a fireplace can be exciting. Most homes built today limit cabinetry to the kitchen, bath, and laundry areas. Built-in living or family room cabinets add charm and functionality to a home. Cabinetry on a fireplace wall can be designed to look like furniture; the difference is that most furniture would not be placed so close to a firebox. When incorporated with a mantel, the focus of the entire room can be enhanced.

PANELING

When creating a wall of millwork without cabinetry, paneling may be the logical choice. Commonly found in upscale and older homes, the additional cost to install wall paneling around a mantel is often prohibitive. Like cabinetry, paneling needs to be designed and installed first. Many of the elements used in paneling can be incorporated into a mantel, such as raised or recessed panels. Paneling can either cover portions of a wall or the entire wall (Figure 333). When covering an entire wall or room with paneling, the paneling becomes the focal point.

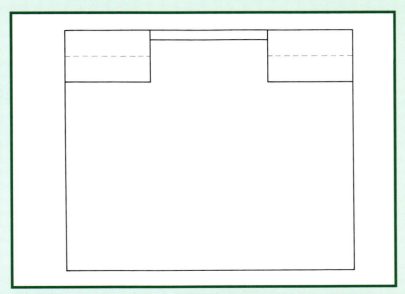

328. Cabinets that are constructed around a flush wall fireplace will project beyond the face of the fireplace. This design can make the fireplace look like it's in a cave. Take care when designing the depth of cabinets, and pay strict attention to the UBC requirements on combustible projections.

329. This fireplace wall is highlighted by oak cabinetry. Before there were cabinets, the room was dominated by brick. Connecting the two pieces of oak cabinetry is a small oak mantelshelf, which serves the secondary purpose of concealing electrical wiring.

330. This simple painted mantel converted a brick face into a slip. It also acts as a bridge between the hickory entertainment center on the right and the display shelving on the left.

331. Painted wood dominates the look of this mantel. Symmetrical pilaster and overmantel paneling enwrap the small shelf. The pink and lavender overmantel crown runs around the entire room.

332. This stately fireplace boasts a yellow marble slip and handcrafted woodcarvings. The wide horizontal stone slip acts as the mantel's frieze. The overmantel envelopes the room on either side with beautiful wall paneling.

333. Book-matched mahogany wood paneling dominates the room. Carrying this theme to the mantel makes the fireplace part of the room rather than isolating it. The recessed alcove is reminiscent of popular Arts and Crafts Inglenook designs.

That much millwork is difficult to downplay with a mantel unless there is juxtaposition with a painted or stone mantel. By introducing different textures of material in this way (juxtapose), the mantel can regain its place as the center of attention. When using the same material, the eye sees the mantel as an element of the paneling, rather than the paneling as an element of the mantel. Therefore, panel layout is critical to the success of the project. Also, make sure you design the mantel to compliment the paneling. If not, it could look like an aberration.

The other application for paneling is to cover a specific area around the mantel. The paneling becomes an extension of the mantel, rather than overtaking it. It can either wrap the mantel or extend just above the mantel shelf. This is commonly referred to as an overmantel. It's an easy way to create a dominant force in the room. Panels above can extend as far as you want. If they extend to the ceiling, additional crown at the ceiling would either stand on the overmantel only, or continue around the room perimeter (Figure 331). The latter application connects the other room elements with the mantel. The same sort of dominant detail could be achieved with a partial height overmantel: one that does not go all the way up to the ceiling (Figure 332). The primary detail difference is that the cap at the top stands alone rather than being part of the room's perimeter crown moulding. This keeps the line of sight below the ceiling, focusing your attention on the mantel wall. Depending on size and design, partial height overmantels can either be built as a separate piece, which is attached to the wall first, or integrated as one piece in the mantel body. Another popular partial paneling application is wainscot. This is a partial height paneling, typically between 3 and 4 feet high, which wraps around a room's perimeter. Wainscot blends well with a fireplace mantel and creates a very elegant look (Figure 333).

Note: There are exceptions to every rule. You may own an older home that has a picture rail in the fireplace room. This is a perimeter moulding like crown or chair rail that installs below the ceiling line on the wall. It was designed to be used for hanging pictures. If this is the case, you may incorporate the picture rail into the cap moulding of a partial height overmantel.

Building either a partial or full-height overmantel lifts the height of the mantel considerably. It now stands like a sentry around the firebox, demanding to be noticed. You don't always need a large room to make this work. The illusion of a higher ceiling can often be created this way if you proportion the height of the cornice shelf properly: too high and it will shrink the ceiling. Bring it as low as possible without crowding the firebox or frieze panel. You can also change the effect by adding a mirror or other design element into the paneling above the mantel.

SECRET PANELS

Hidden compartments in a mantel are both practical and fun. Mantel construction allows the addition of secret spaces. But they must be worked into the initial design, not added as an afterthought. If the secret compartment is a unique element it will draw attention to itself and thus defeat its purpose. The secret compartments I have designed are typically incorporated into a panel. Although these can be added to any type of mantel, they are least noticeable in mantels finished with clear finishing products. You can add one on a painted mantel, but it will be more noticeable because all joints will be caulked except for the perimeter of the secret door. Any cracks or exposed joints in a painted mantel are pronounced by a shadow line and lack of paint. It can, however, be pulled off with careful planning.

It's simplest to integrate a secret compartment on an applied panel mantel (Figure 335). The panels are overlaid on the surround and invite the least amount of attention. To fabricate a secret compartment, an opening will need to be cut into the pilaster or frieze behind the applied panel. Construct a box to fit inside the pilaster. Consider the size of the door opening when building your box. Don't plan on a large, deep compartment if the door size restricts what will fit. The panel or door needs a concealed hinge to open. I like to use 35 mm cup hinges. They install easily and provide three-way adjustment (Figure 336) that makes it easy to adjust

334. Wainscot is a popular wall treatment. When used in a room with a mantel, both millwork pieces support each other. Notice the mitered effect between the pilaster and frieze.

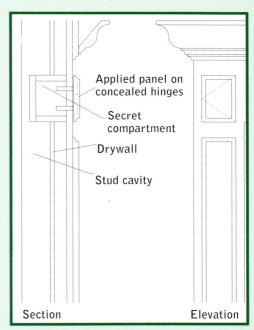

Applied panel on concealed hinges

Secret compartment

Drywall

Stud cavity

Section   Elevation

335. Secret space can be created by hinging one panel with concealed hinges.

Concealed Hinges

Concealed hinges have revolutionized the cabinet door-hanging industry. With the ease of installation and the wide range of adjustability, success for this hardware was imminent. At first glance, concealed hinges appear complicated to install, but are really very easy. Since I frequently use these hinges, I have a dedicated drilling press. For the occasional user, you'll need a 35 mm drill bit. Locate the placement on the door. Take half the distance to the center of the 35 mm hole (which is about 11/16 inch) and add 3/16 inch, to give you 7/8 inch to the center of the hinge cup hole. Drill to a depth of 1/2 inch. Insert and attach the hinge. You should have a 3/16-inch space from the door edge to the hinge edge (Figure 337). The beauty of the concealed hinge is its adjustability. Three screws adjust the movement of vertical, horizontal, and in and out movement (photo 336). This is a real plus when lining up a concealed panel.

336. Concealed cup hinges offer three-way adjustment. #1 moves the door horizontally. #2 moves the door in and out. #3 adjusts the door up and down.

337. Most concealed cup hinges require the same door preparation: 35mm cup hole and a setback from the door edge of approximately 3/16 inch.

338. For hidden door panels you need a hidden mechanism that allows the door to open without a pull or knob. The mechanical touch-latch on the left offers the most rigid connection. Magnetic touch-latches as shown in the center are easy to install but depend on the magnet's strength to hold the panel closed. The push latch on the left uses a heavy spring that makes it a good choice for pushing heavy drawers open.

the door so it looks just like the adjacent panels. If you use self-closing hinges, no mechanism is needed to hold the door shut. I prefer free-swinging hinges, which have no spring installed, meaning they need a door catch to keep the door shut. A mechanical touch latch works the best because it latches the door firmly in place (Figure 338 left). Magnetic latches are another option but they can be pulled open easily (Figure 338 center), a potential problem with inadvertent handling. Although this method leaves a small gap (required by the hinge and touch latch to work), it is fairly inconspicuous and is very easy to fabricate.

Another panel door option is designing the mantel with a series of flush inset panel units (Figure 339). Each panel could be detailed with frame and panel construction, along with a beaded insert. This would allow enough reveals to easily conceal a secret panel. Construction would be the same as for an applied panel. The main difference is that you probably have to use a free-swinging hinge with a touch latch, because a self-closing hinge on a flush inset door would be impossible to open without a knob, not an option for a mantel.

You could even incorporate a sliding panel for a secret compartment door. It's a little more difficult to fabricate, but it is very inconspicuous. I've done this with other recessed, flat-panel designs. Since the panel has to slide behind the pilaster, you must decide where it will slide to. Sliding panels on a pilaster will dictate a vertical movement. Do you want the panel to slide up or down? There are pros and cons to each method.

To slide the panel down, the bottom panel in a pilaster is the best option (Figure 340). The panel can be recessed to the same depth as the other panels in the pilaster, since there are no other panels below it; that is the greatest advantage to this option. Before gluing up the frame, modify the bottom rail so its thickness is the same as the recess depth. This will allow the panel to slide down into the groove cut in the vertical stile for the panel.

Note: The panel recess dimension is typically 1/4 inch to 3/8 inch when using 3/4-inch frame construction. When building a sliding door, use at least a 3/8-inch recessed dimension so you can adequately attach the false rail. A biscuit is the best method for securing this rail. Add a full 3/4-inch rail below the false rail to give the pilaster bottom more strength. Take care not to nail through the false rail when attaching the base.

The disadvantage to this method is getting the panel to stay in place. You'll have to design a mechanism that will prevent it from sliding down on its own. One way would be with an inconspicuous pin located on the side of the pilaster. Simply pull out the pin to release the door. Add a dummy pin on the opposite side so the real pin does not attract attention.

The other option is to slide the panel up (Figure 341). If you have enough room at the top and there are no other panels in the same plane above, then this would be a preferred method. Employ the same method of construction as

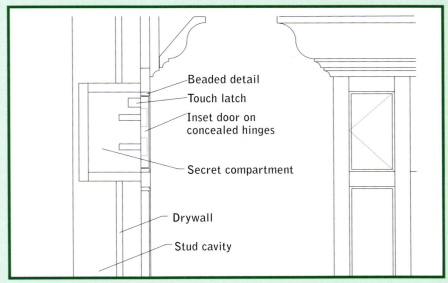

339. Inset panels also lend themselves well to creating a secret panel. Although a visible line at the opening will be seen, it may not be noticed. The key to avoiding detection is making all the panels look the same.

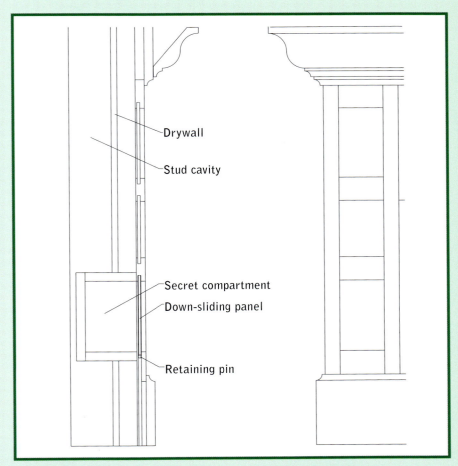

340. Sliding panels can also be incorporated, such as this down-sliding option. The panel groove on the stile acts as the track. Because the panel slides down, a retaining pin must be used to hold the panel in place.

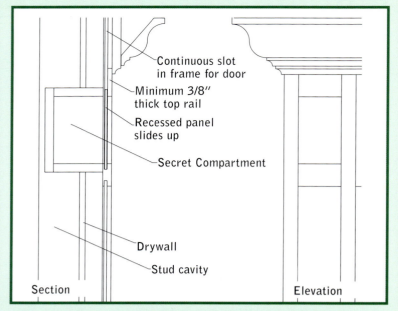

Section   Elevation

341. Up-sliding secret panels have the advantage of gravity keeping the operable panel in place. It is important to make sure the panel slides smoothly in the channel; panels that bind are going to be difficult to move.

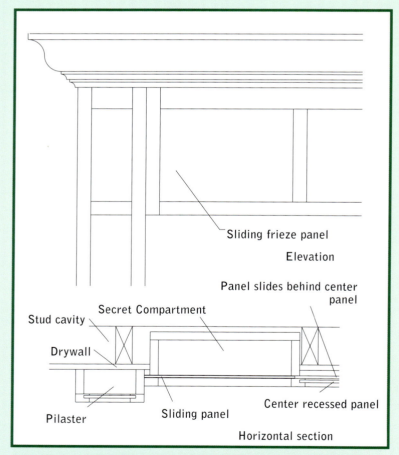

342. Horizontal sliding panels require different detailing than their vertical cousins. Adjacent fixed panels must be offset in order for the moveable panel to have a place to go.

described above, only this time use the upper pilaster panel. With a panel sliding up, you never have to worry about it coming open on its own since gravity will hold it in place. However, some mantel designs won't allow enough room at the top for this. It's easier if you can keep the sliding parts confined to the same mantel component (i.e. pilaster or frieze).

A sliding panel can be incorporated in the frieze. This panel would need to slide horizontally (Figure 342). Gravity is kind to the sliding frieze panel as well. The key to designing either type of sliding panel is making it inconspicuous. If the panel has to slide behind adjacent panels, it must be recessed deeper in the frame. Recess the opposite dummy panel the same way to keep the details consistent.

Other methods include the swinging pilaster (Figure 343), which is not for the faint-hearted. It requires significantly more engineering and would be attempted only where needs dictate a larger secret space. Much like secret room access in a bookshelf, the swinging pilaster provides greater space. If you have incorporated wall paneling with the mantel, this may be the location of choice. Panels provide better size and joinery options for secret inclusion of a wall safe.

There are many variations of the secret compartment, and a little ingenuity is all that's required. Each mantel design is unique and will require special modification to accommodate a secret space. Attention to detail can make it a prized addition.

DUMMY MANTELS

Dummy mantels simulate a mantel in design, but are not located around a fireplace. One example would be a mantel built to house a television in an entertainment center. It could have all the visual attributes of a mantel, but a nontraditional use. Because mantels are attractive millwork pieces, they lend themselves to many applications. I've made dummy mantels for bedroom walls with no fireplace. It's amazing how a mantel recreates the cozy feeling of snuggling up to a fire. A full mantel surround could stand alone as display shelving. Even wall-mounted shelving can have details of cornice and frieze to enhance its appearance. Thinking only of a fireplace application will limit your vision of a mantels use.

In recent years, mantel design has found its way into the kitchen. Long ago, when people cooked in their fireplaces, they often had a lintel or a decorative mantel that kitchen implements were stored on. Now, the mantel design elements of pilaster, frieze, cornice, and overmantel can be seen around the stove of many upscale kitchens. Early mantels suggested practical and functional uses for the modern kitchen designer to incorporate in a kitchen mantel. Instead of concealing the large expanse of a chimney, kitchen mantels today use a frieze to conceal the stoves exhaust fan. These mantel range hoods can also hold cooking utensils and spices in pilaster-type paneled doors. Even a cornice shelf can be incorporated to display objects of interest (Fig-ure 324, page 178).

A mantel's design lends itself well to many creative applications. It has a recognizable appearance that is timeless. Don't think you must have a fireplace in your home to enjoy a mantel. If you let creativity dominate the logical side of your mind, you'll find a way to incorporate the mantel's distinctive elements as solutions to design challenges presented in other woodworking projects. ●

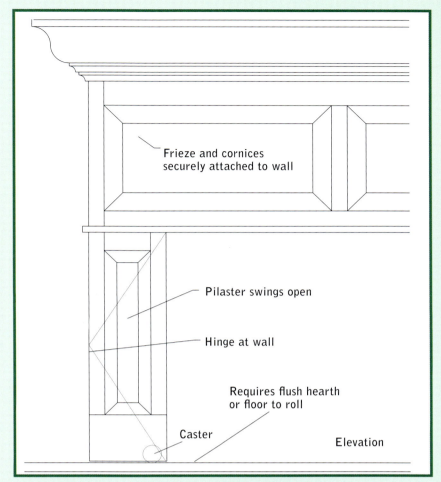

Frieze and cornices securely attached to wall

Pilaster swings open

Hinge at wall

Requires flush hearth or floor to roll

Caster

Elevation

343. For the mechanically inclined individual who needs (or wants) a larger secret space in the mantel, the entire pilaster can be designed to swivel out. A concealed hinge system to prevent discovery will be needed. Depending on size, a caster at the bottom may be required for smooth operation.

344. Power feeders enhance safety. Feeders keep the operator's hands safely away from the cutter, allowing better concentration on the work. They also provide consistent speed and pressure, resulting in cleaner cuts. Along with the power feeder, wear a dust mask, eye and ear protection, and stand alongside the line of cut, not in the path of a kickback.

Shop Safety

NO DISCUSSION OF FABRICATION techniques would be complete without touching on safety. Living itself is inherently dangerous. When you introduce sharp tooling, heavy materials, and hand/eye coordination of the two, you increase the level of peril to your body. Much like an athlete training for an event, the woodworker must also prepare for his opponent. The difference is that the opponent is inanimate; it cannot defeat you or harm you unless you flip the switch. However, it is present every time you enter the shop. Since it does not think, it has no concern for you. The battle is in your own mind. Therefore, the best way to defend yourself against accidents in the shop is to be as fully informed as possible. Know your tools. Start by reading their instructions. Know what a tool is designed for and what its limitations are. Know your materials. Understanding the characteristics of different materials will help you make an informed, hence safe decision on how to process material. You also must understand the process of fabrication so you can make wise machining choices. You don't have to be an expert, just a good student. Reading books, talking to experts, and above all, spending time in your shop practicing with your tools is the best way to prepare yourself.

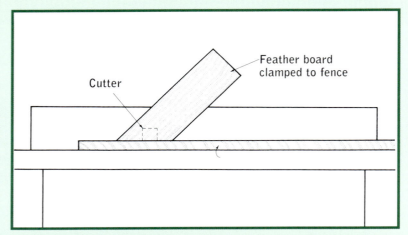

345. A feather board or other hold-down device keeps material tight against the fence and cutter. This results in cleaner cuts, and allows you to keep hands at a safe distance.

Cutter

Feather board clamped to fence

346. Eye protection comes in a wide variety of choices. Full-face shields (right) offer protection for the entire face; goggles (top) encapsulate the eyes for maximum defense; safety glasses (middle and bottom left) are available in many styles.

347. Protecting your ears from noisy machinery enhances concentration on the work at hand. The best protection is the full ear headset (left). Disposable earplugs come in a variety of styles and colors to suit individual tastes.

Tools are the first things that come to mind regarding a discussion on safety. After twenty professional years behind the saw, I have developed a greater respect for tools than when I started out. Remembering one simple principle will give you all the respect for tools you need: if it cuts wood, plastic, or stone, it will cut flesh. The most common power tools used in mantel fabrication will be the table saw, router, biscuit cutter, and drill motor. Either use the guards that came with the machine, or make guards of your own.

Covering a blade or bit is cheap insurance. Always use a push stick when the piece you are milling is too small. To avoid getting hit by a piece of wood that kicks back, never stand directly behind the table saw blade. Resist the temptation to press material down or against a blade or bit. Use hold downs instead so your hands stay clear of the cutting tools (Figure 345). Better yet, if you have a power feeder, use it ((Figure 344, page 188). Another important guide is to never perform an operation you are unfamiliar with, or one that generates fear. Confidence in technique is one of the keys to safe tool operation. That's why you need a basic understanding of joinery, both in application and fabrication. Since what you will learn in this text only covers the basics, take classes or study books to gain knowledge.

Eye protection cannot be over emphasized. We have only been given two eyes to guide us through life, so take good care of them. Unlike the generic safety glasses found in school shop classes of yesteryear, there are a wide array of safety glasses on the market today that offer good protection, fit, and appearance. If the prescription glasses you wear do not have safety glass, goggles or a full-face visor are good options (Figure 346). Unlike glasses, goggles protect the side of the eye. Full-face visors go a step further by providing protection to the entire face.

Noise and dust are two additional factors in the safety issue. The obvious damage to unprotected ears and lungs is only part of the consideration. Continuous loud noise makes it difficult to concentrate. Routers and shapers operate at a high decibel level. Because they spin with a high revolution per minute (rpm) in a circular motion, cutters can pull a piece in or shoot it out like a bullet, depending on the direction of feed. Therefore, a high level of concentration is required. To gain confident use of loud tools, always use ear plugs or headsets (Figure 347). Both work well in preventing injury to the ears. Use whichever feels more comfortable. Again, limiting the amount of exposure to dangerous noise lessens the chance of an accident.

Dust is another safety concern for today's woodworker. The first line of defense is the source. Connect your tools to dust collectors or vacuums. Much of the debris they pick up, however, will be the larger wood chips (unless you have a sophisticated system). It's the fine dust particles that you can't see that are the most dangerous: you breathe these particles into your lungs. Down-draft tables

348. Dust masks keep small, airborne dust particles out of the lungs. Inexpensive, single-strap masks (left), or better quality double-strap varieties (right) are the first line of defense.

are great for fine dust collection during sanding operations. They've been around for quite a while in commercial settings, but are now showing up in most tool catalogs since the dangers of dust inhalation have been exposed. My shop uses a combination of a dust collector and a continuous running forced air filter. The dust collector picks up the larger particles. The air filtering system recycles the shop air while collecting the fine particles. Although I have noticed a significant difference in air quality since this was installed, the problem has not been totally eliminated. On a day when the sunshine extends its rays into the workspace, you can see fine particles that escaped filtering. These remind me of the dangers of airborne dust. It's for that reason I still use a dust mask when performing dust-generating operations. Many dust masks are available. I like disposable ones that use two bands to secure the mask on your face (Figure 348). It's important to get a good seal,

349. When working with most wood finishes, a good quality organic vapor respirator is a must. Partial facemasks are the most common (right). Full-face masks (left) help keep vapors out of the eyes. Filters must be replaced regularly.

350. Disposable paint suits help keep clothes clean. Finishes, especially sprayed finishes, adhere to skin, hair and clothing. Keeping overspray off your body is an important safety consideration.

351. Many finishers don't like wearing gloves because they claim it is harder to control a hand-wiped product. Toxic chemicals, however, can enter the body through skin, so proper precautions should be taken. For extreme chemicals and sensitive hands, there is the chemical rated rubber glove (left). The best all-around glove is the industrial nitrile glove (center). Latex rubber, the most common, should only be used for latex products.

and your lungs deserve the protection. Don't buy a mask based on price alone. The less expensive masks are thinner, use only one band, and don't seal as well, allowing dust to bypass them (Figure 348). For the best protection against dust, some manufacturers sell a full-face mask complete with a pump that re-circulates its own air, a great idea for those sensitive to dust.

It can be easy to forget about wearing a dust mask since you often don't see the dust, and the smell is usually not offensive. This is not the case with wood finishes. Even when you don't see the fumes of a toxic finish, its smell is usually enough to make you realize you need protection. For wood finishes you'll need to invest in a few specialty safety products. First, a good organic vapor rated mask is a must (Figure 349). These are available in partial or full-face protection. A dust mask will not adequately keep fumes from your lungs. Also, check the cartridge specifications. Some are rated only for latex products.

Your next consideration is a set of coveralls with a hood (Figure 350). Coveralls not only protect your clothing from overspray and spillage, but also keep toxic material away from your skin. Purchase rubber gloves as well. There are several different types. The standard latex glove commonly used in the medical field is good for general protection and for use with latex products. These fit snugly and are least noticeable. They will, however, disintegrate with oil-based products. The industrial

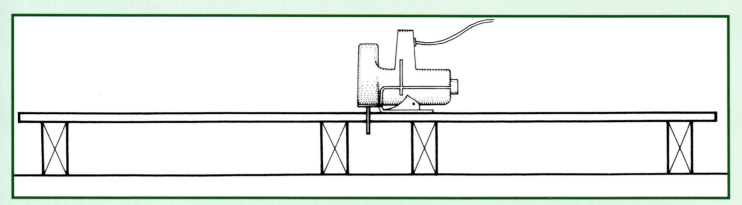

352. Cutting sheet goods on the ground requires good support on both sides of the blade, preventing the material from binding the blade and getting damaged.

nitrile rubber glove is slightly more expensive, but they offer superior protection with oil-based products. In addition, they are thin enough to still feel the material under your fingertips, unlike the third type, the heavy duty chemical rated rubber glove (Figure 351). These protect best against chemical dangers, but are bulky. In fact, they probably provide more protection than you'll need for finishing work.

The final item for your finishing safety kit is common sense. Never use toxic or flammable products in closed areas or near flames. This includes pilot lights on stoves and furnaces. Several years ago I was working in a home that was being remodeled. One morning the painter sprayed an epoxy finish in the bathroom. By the time I arrived, the whole house was filled with toxic fumes. There were no fans or other attempts to recycle the air. I took a journey down to the basement where the painter was working and was greatly surprised to see him working in that bathroom without even a vapor mask! When I talked to him about it later, he calmly lit up a cigarette and said, "I'm a painter. I'm used to

it." Never substitute laziness for common sense. Use protective clothing and always work in a well-ventilated area.

Materials are another safety topic. Sheet goods such as plywood, MDF, particleboard, etc., are heavy and awkward and can be hard to control. It's easy to knock things over when moving a sheet around, especially when working in a small space. Proper lifting techniques, like using your knees instead of your back, go a long way in reducing back injury. An extra set of hands also reduces the stress on your body. For safely cutting sheet goods, you'll need good support for the material. If working with a hand-held circular saw, use saw horses to support the material both before and after the cut. This way, the cut-off doesn't fall and get damaged, or harm you. Working at table height rather than on the ground is much easier on your back. Excessive bending causes premature fatigue. If you must work on the ground, place blocking under a sheet good on either end and under the line of cut. This will support the board all the way through the cut and protect the saw blade from damage

353. Safe cutting on the table saw requires adequate support of the material both on the in-feed and out-feed sides. As shown in the photo, the best support is a firm table. Portable rollers can also be used.

(Figure 352). If cutting on a table saw, you must have in-feed and out-feed support (Figure 353). In a pinch, you can rely on your hand as the in-feed support and a helper as the out-feed. A simple fixed table or roller, however, will give you better control, equating superior accuracy and hence safety. Without out-feed support, the sheet good will start to drop once its center point crosses the blade. You don't want to support the weight from the in-feed side of the table saw. This is extremely dangerous. Even when using a bench model saw that is close to the ground, it's still very unsafe. Bench saws will actually tip over without adequate out-feed support. Solid wood, although lighter and easier to manage, will also need support, particularly when cutting boards longer than 8 feet. A simple rule of thumb is: the longer and heavier the board, the more support it is going to need.

Choose clothing carefully. Loose clothing and hanging jewelry should not be worn; nor should anything you don't have control over while using tools. Loose items can easily get pulled into spinning blades or bits. While gloves provide protection against splinters and chaffing, be certain to exercise caution when using gloves. Hands are typically the body part that comes closest to blades and cutters. Large, loose fitting gloves are not recommended. A good-fitting pair of leather gloves will last the longest and offers the best protection. Even disposable latex gloves provide surprising defense from hand wear, and are relatively safe because of their snug fit.

Experience gives you more confidence in a process, but does not guarantee a safe process. Sometimes we lose common sense when we gain experience because of the confidence we have developed. A beginning woodworker crosses the line of safety when he does something he does not understand. A professional slips up when he performs an unsafe operation based on his familiarity with the tool. Accidents occur to the novice and experienced alike and know no distinction between the two. Therefore, always exercise common sense when working with tools. This is best done by respecting the tools, not being afraid of them. Most accidents can be prevented if we are aware of the dangers that can happen, and take steps to prevent them. The shop is not the place to get lazy. Save that for when you go to bed. ●

Sources of Supply

ASSOCIATIONS
- Architectural Woodworking Institute — www.awinet.org
- Cabinet Makers Association — www.cabinetmakers.org
- The Hardwood Council — www.hardwoodcouncil.com
- The Furniture Society — www.furnituresociety.org

CAST STONE MANTELS
- Old world Stoneworks, Dallas, TX — 800-600-8336

COLUMNS AND ACCESSORIES
- Worthington, Troy, AL — 800-872-1608

COMPOSITE MOULDINGS AND ACCESSORIES
- RAS Industries, Charleroi, PA — 800-367-1076
- Outwater Plastics Industries, Inc., Wood Ridge, NJ — 800-631-8375

CULTURED MARBLE
- Designer's Marble, Woodinville, WA — 800-310-5940

FLEXIBLE MOULDINGS
- Flex Moulding, Inc., Hackensack, NJ — 201-487-8080
- Flex Trim Industries, Cucamonga, CA — 909-944-6665

GENERAL WOODWORKING SUPPLIES
- Woodworker's Warehouse, Amesbury, MA — 781-598-2000
- Rockler Woodworking, Medina, MN — 763-478-8262
- Woodcraft Supply, Parkersburg, WV — 304-442-5412
- Lee Valley Tools, Ottawa, ON Canada — 613-596-0350

HARDWOOD LUMBER AND VENEERS
- Eisenbrand, Inc., Torrance, CA — 800-258-2587
- Flamingo Specialty Veneers, East Orange NJ — 973-672-7600
- CertainlyWood Inc., East Aurora NY — 716-655-0206
- MacBeath Hardwoods, Berkeley CA — 510-843-4390
- Austin Hardwoods, Santa Ana, CA — 714-953-4000

MOULDINGS
- Architectural Wood Mouldings, Waterloo , Ontario Canada   519-884-4080
- Arvid's Woods, Lynnwood, WA   800-627-8437
- Executive Woodsmiths, Charlotte, NC   800-951-9090
- Hillsdale Sash and Door, Issaquah, WA   877-209-2054

PRE-FORMED PLYWOOD CYLINDERS
- B&D International, Tacoma, WA   800-222-7853
- L.I. Laminates, Inc., Hauppauge, NY   800-221-5454

SOLID SURFACE MATERIALS
- Dupont Corian   800-4CORIAN

SOLID WOOD TURNINGS AND COMPONENTS
- Adams Wood Products, Morristown, TN   423-587-2942

SPECIALTY DECORATIVE MOULDINGS AND CARVINGS
- Artistic Woodworking, Imperial, NE   308-882-4873
- Bendix Mouldings, Inc, Northvale, NJ   800-526-0240
- Braided Accents   www.braidedaccents.com
- Raymond Enkeboll Designs, Carson, CA   310-532-1400

WOOD STAINS AND FINISHES
- Woodworker's Supply, Casper, WY   800-645-9292
- Daly's Inc., Seattle WA   206-633-4200

Flutes:
    router jig for, 135
    stopped, 54
    stopped, 136-137
    through, 55
Form, as design element, 19
Frame-and-panel, defined, 116
French cleat, for installations, 176-177
Frieze:
    curved, 23
    defined, 16, 18
    placement of, 18
    secret compartment in, 186
    skeleton for, 131-132, 134
    straight, 23
    width of, 27

Gaps, caulk for, 172, 175
Georgian style, 12
Gloves, for finishing, 192
Glue:
    applying with brush, 104
    drying time of, 110
    for miters, 130
    for panels, 127
    in biscuit joints, 102
Glue size, as sealer, 154
Golden section, defined, 19

Hammer drill, for masonry, 171
Head blocks, defined, 55-56
Header, defined, 16
Hearth:
    and pilasters, 21
    defined, 16
    raised, 21
    types of, 20-21
Hidden compartments, in mantel,
    183-187
Hinges, for secret compartments,
    183-184
Hold-downs, importance of, 190
HVLP, spray gear, 161

Installation:
    and prefab fireplace, 166
    of mantel, 163-177
    sequence of, 113
Italian tile:
    fireplace of, 78
    ornate mantel of, 81

Jamb, defined, 16
Jigsaw, for scribing mantel, 172
Jointing lumber, for flatness, 119

Keystones, defined, 59
Kick back, avoiding, 190

Lacquer finish, application of, 157
Level:
    for installations, 167
    using, 35
Light, as design element, 19
Line, as design element, 19
Lintel:
    defined, 11
    defined, 16
    early, 12

Mahogany mantel:
    with cabinetry, 94
    with Inglenook, 95
    with ormolu mounts, 83
Makore veneers, mantel of, 80
Mantel:
    antique, 25
    as home's heartbeat, 15
    defined, 11
    early, 12
    fastening methods, 39
    in kitchen, 178, 187
    materials for, 14
Mantel parts:
    component assembly of, 43
    fabrication of, 43
Mantel shelf:
    19th century, 13
    contemporary, 18
    defined, 11
    defined, 16
    depth of, 27
    gluing in place, 174
    scribing to wall, 173
Maple mantel:
    virtues of, 47-48
    with pre-fab fireplace, 94
    with round pilasters, 87
Measuring, techniques of, 35
Medium-density fiberboard:
    types of, 45-46, 49
    virtues of, 49
Medium-density overlay, virtues of,
    48
Mirror, in overmantel, 13, 14
Mistakes, correcting, 164
Miters:
    for crown moulding, 141-142, 145
    sawing of, 108-110, 128-129
    virtues of, 128
Mock-up, as design tool, 28-29
Moisture content, of wood, 99
Moisture meter, use of, 99
Mouldings:
    applied, 120
    buy versus make, 116
    carved, 57

Mouldings (continued)
    cope and stick, 120
    cutting sequence, 119
    defined, 51
    egg-and-dart, 57
    for panels, 53-54
    of plastic, 49
    samples of, 38
    symmetric, 54
    to fill gaps, 174-175
    types of, 51-59
    wood species for, 44
Moving methods, for mantels, 165

Nail holes, putty for, 175
Nailer, pneumatic, 109
Natural stone, virtues of, 66-67
Non-combustible materials, dimen-
    sions of, 27
Non-combustible slip, materials for,
    63-70

Oak mantel, with oak cabinetry, 93
Oil finish, application of, 156
Overmantel:
    defined, 12, 16
Overmantel, design of, 182-183
Overmantel, height of, 27, 183

Paint finish:
    application of, 159
    preparation for, 159
    types of, 159
Painted mantel:
    of MDF, 115
    with brick slip, 92
    with cabinets, 84
    with corbels, 82
    with dentil trim, 85
    with fluted pilasters, 89
    with mouldings, 80
    with wainscot, 88
Panel:
    back cut for, 126
    cutting sequence for, 126-127
    defined, 116
    grain direction of, 107
    mouldings for, 53
    raised, 117
    recessed, 117
    squareness of, 127
    with mantel, 181-182
    with rabbet, 117
Panel clips, for installations, 176
Particleboard, types of, 45-46, 49
Parting bead, defined, 56
Pediment, defined, 16